BROOKHAVEN BINDERY 06559
PH. 608-781-0850 ext. 222
2004 Kramer St.
La Crosse, WI 54603

Customer	ALLEN COUNTY PUBLIC LIBRARY		
Cust. No.	BHP	RUB NO.	S2
Lot No.	137	SIZE	10 5/8 Lines NO
P.O. No.	HW0599	COLOR	598 GOLD

Total

Over 2 1/2

Collating

Stubbing　　　H.C.

Filling

SUGGESTIVE PLANS
FOR INDIANA'S
CENTENNIAL CELEBRATION

1912

SPECIAL INSTRUCTIONS

TARGET 7
FRT.8 1/2

Number of vols. 1

Notify

Deliver

Mail　X

Suggestive Plans for Indiana's Centennial
Celebration, 1916

_____

This is an exact reproduction of an original book.
Any errors that exist in the original, including typographic
errors and errors in pagination, exist in this facsimile.

Digital Production by
Northern Micrographics, A Division of NMT Corporation
La Crosse, Wisconsin
Copyright 2001 NMT Corporation
www.nmt.com

Published by
Brookhaven Press, A Division of NMT Corporation
La Crosse, Wisconsin
www.brookhavenpress.com 1.800.236.0850

HW0599 IN0610
ISBN 1-4035-0051-7

Indiana Centennial Celebration Committee

Dr. Frank B. Wynn, Chairman
311 Newton Claypool Building, Indianapolis

FIRST DISTRICT
John W. Spencer, Evansville
Judge Supreme Court of Indiana

SECOND DISTRICT
Wm. L. Bryan, Bloomington
President Indiana University

THIRD DISTRICT
Lew M. O'Bannon, Corydon
Editor and Proprietor the Corydon Democrat

FOURTH DISTRICT
I. Newt Brown, Franklin
President State Board of Agriculture

FIFTH DISTRICT
Albert O. Lockridge, Greencastle
Farmer and Lecturer on Agricultural Topics

SIXTH DISTRICT
Dr. Samuel E. Smith, Richmond
Medical Supt. Eastern Indiana Hospital for Insane

SEVENTH DISTRICT
Cassius C. Hadley, Indianapolis
Ex-Judge of the Appellate Court of Indiana

Johf E. Hollett, Indianapolis
Ex-President Commercial Club of Indianapolis

EIGHTH DISTRICT
W. H. Eichhorn, Bluffton
Circuit Judge 28th Judicial Circuit

NINTH DISTRICT
Dan Waugh, Tipton
Ex-Congressman

TENTH DISTRICT
Winthrop E. Stone, Lafayette
President Purdue University

ELEVENTH DISTRICT
W. H. Sanders, Marion
Editor Marion Daily Chronicle

TWELFTH DISTRICT
Andrew A. Adams, Columbia City
Judge of the Appellate Court of Indiana

THIRTEENTH DISTRICT
Dr. Edward A. Rumely, Laporte
Treasurer and General Manager M. Rumely Co.

Table of Contents

		PAGE
1.	Scope and Character of the Proposed Celebration. By the Committee	9

Let it be conducted along Historical and Educational lines, in which every community is participant.

2. The Indiana Centennial Commission. Demarchus Brown, Secretary Commission 16

   Its purpose, to select site and prepare plans for a Memorial Library and Museum. In addition, there should be an adequate and appropriate celebration.

3. Growth and Achievements of the Law. Addison C. Harris 19

   An historical review with suggestions as to how the evolution of Indiana's laws may best be shown.

4. Religion. Francis H. Gavisk and M. L. Haines 25

   What religion has been to the settlement and development of the State, and suggestions as to how this might be set forth in the celebration.

5. Indiana History and Its Celebration. James A. Woodburn, Indiana University 30

   Showing how the whole history of the State might be told impressively in pageantry; also an argument for historical research and the preservation of historical material.

6. Literature. Meredith Nicholson 38

   Besides the historical pageant it is recommended that a department be devoted in the new Library and Museum to Indiana literature and relics pertaining to its development.

7. Elementary Education. Charles A. Greathouse, Superintendent of Public Instruction 45

   Traces the development of the school building, text-books, school equipment, modifications in school discipline, etc., showing how exhibits could be made highly instructive.

8. Collegiate Education in Indiana. William L. Bryan, President Indiana University 51

   Outline suggesting collection of books, and pictures, and the preparation of charts, and the presentation of lectures, setting forth the history and progress of institutions of learning.

9. Music. Edward B. Birge 55

   Preparations should be begun at once in all the larger towns and cities for a great Music Fest in 1916. Long preparatory training will be essential for a successful musical event.

10. Art. Frederick Allen Whiting, Director Herron Art Institute, Indianapolis 58

    State has achieved worthily in art, and some of the best men amongst the Indiana group should be chosen to make the mural decorations in the Library and Museum; and the Hoosier spirit should be exemplified in a splendid sculptural group.

11. Outline of an Exhibit of Technical Education. Winthrop E. Stone, President Purdue University 63

    The technical schools of the State would be able to contribute largely toward a centennial celebration, since work of this kind lends itself well for purposes of demonstration.

12. Agriculture. G. I. Christie, Purdue University 67

    Show by scientifically demonstrated exhibits the agricultural resources and possibilities of the State.

PAGE

13. Forestry. Stanley Coulter, Purdue University.................... 71
    Exhibits should set forth lucidly what we originally had, what we have and what we might have.

14. Public Health. J. N. Hurty, Secretary State Board of Health...... 73
    In the celebration health exhibits would teach the lessons of preventable diseases; the need of keeping streams pure, of better hygiene for towns and cities, and of fostering school-hygiene.

15. Outline of Proposed Athletic Events. T. F. Moran and Hugh Nicol, Purdue University 77
    Show history of development of athletics in State and provide finally in the celebration for a great Olympic.

16. Civic Coordination and Park Development. Henry Jameson, President Indianapolis Park Board........................... 81
    Make survey of cities and towns of State with a view to stimulating civic betterment, æsthetic, hygienic and sanitary.

17. Charities and Correction. Amos W. Butler, Secretary State Board of Charities 87
    History and progress of Indiana's charitable and penal institutions and methods; how they may best be shown in the celebration.

18. Suggestions for a Display of Indiana's Minerals, Fossils, Quarries, etc. David Worth Dennis, Earlham College.................... 95
    Such an exhibition could not only be made very attractive, but very instructive and practical.

19. Stock and Farming Resources. Charles Downing, Secretary State Board of Agriculture 99
    Exhibition would reveal our vast resources and, scientifically presented, would give tremendous impetus to better stock raising and farming methods.

20. Manufactures, Commerce and Trade. Edward A. Rumely, Laporte.. 103
    A Historical and Educational Celebration would unify the divided interests and regions of Indiana, making for a greater future—commercial, cultural and moral.

21. Transportation. Clarence A. Kenyon, Indianapolis................ 110
    Development in Indiana. Exhibits properly demonstrated would teach lessons about road building and many other subjects relating to transportation.

22. How to Awaken General Interest in the Centennial Celebration. Lew M. O'Bannon, Corydon 119
    Reach people by a booklet in the schools, recounting Indiana's history and achievements. Every community should participate somehow in the celebration.

23. Convention Hall, Indianapolis. Henry R. Danner and L. H. Lewis.. 122
    An adequate convention hall in Indianapolis is a pressing need for the city and State, which must and will be met by the public spirited citizenship of Indianapolis in ample time for the Centennial Celebration.

24. Going Back Home in 1916. Wilbur D. Nesbit, Chicago............ 125
    To visit again the old scenes and grasp again the hands of old friends, will be the rarest privilege which all ex-Hoosiers will enjoy in the home-coming.

25. Quotations from a Few Letters Relating to the Proposed Centennial Celebration in 1916.. 133

26. Newer Buildings of Indiana Colleges............................ 136

27. Illustrations Showing Progress and Development in Various Fields.. 140

List of Illustrations

		Page
1.	Soldiers' and Sailors' Monument	8
2.	First State House, Corydon	10
3.	Second State House, Indianapolis	12
4.	Postoffice, Indianapolis, 1850	14
5.	Present Postoffice Building, Indianapolis	15
6.	Cartoon showing necessity for more room in State House	16
7.	Present Indiana State House	17
8.	Indiana Territorial Government House, Vincennes	20
9.	First Governor of Indiana	21
10.	Tippecanoe Battle Ground	22
11.	Little Cedar Church, near Brookville	25
12.	McKendrie Church, near Brookville	26
13.	Henry Ward Beecher's Church	28
14.	St. Mary's Catholic Church, Indianapolis	29
15.	Pioneer Hoosier Residence	32
16.	Indiana Residence of 1840	32
17.	Group of Modern Residences	34
18.	Maps of Early Indiana	36
19.	Edward Eggleston	38
20.	Edward Eggleston's Birthplace	39
21.	General Lew Wallace	40
22.	Interior of Lew Wallace's Study	42
23.	Exterior of Lew Wallace's Study	43
24.	First Log Schoolhouse in Wayne County	45
25.	Little Red Schoolhouse	46
26.	Recent Type of Country Schoolhouse	47
27.	Consolidated High School Building	48
28.	First Buildings of Indiana Colleges	50
29.	First Building Indiana University	52
30.	Early Buildings Asbury University	53
31.	"On the Banks of the Wabash Far Away"	55
32.	Noblesville Band, 1850	56
33.	Herron Art Institute, Indianapolis	58
34.	Exhibition Art Work, Richmond	59
35.	Exhibit of Student Art Work	60
36.	Purdue School of Mechanical Engineering	62
37.	Purdue Agricultural Building	64
38.	The Purdue Herd	66
39.	What Indiana Might Do for Apple Production	68
40.	Giant White Oak	70
41.	Rocky Mountain Forest and an Indiana Woods	72
43.	Indiana Tuberculosis Hospital	74
44.	Protect Indiana Streams	75
45.	Public Swimming Pool	78
46.	Public Playground	79
47.	A Beautiful Stream to Conserve	82
48.	An Old Wooden Bridge	83
49.	A New Indiana Bridge	84
50.	Before and After Treatment by a Park Board	85
51.	Proposed State House Plaza	86
52.	Early Type of Indiana Jail	87
53.	State Prison, Michigan City	88
54.	Old Orange County Infirmary	90
55.	New Orange County Infirmary	91
56.	Administration Building, Northern Hospital for Insane	93
57.	An Indiana Quarry	95
58.	Skeleton of a Mastodon	96
59.	"Shades of Death"	97
60.	Indiana-bred Horses	99
61.	Model Dairy Barn	100
62.	Indiana Prize-winning Cow	101

		Page
63.	Tunnel Mill near Vernon	104
64.	Indiana-made Tractor and Plows	105
65.	Center of Population of the United States	106
66.	Old State Bank, Brookville	107
67.	Ox-team in Transportation	111
68.	Packet "Governor Morton," First Trip	112
69.	First Gasoline Motor Vehicle in United States	113
70.	The Indianapolis Motor Speedway	114
71.	Up-to-date Railway Transportation	116
72.	"The Constitutional Elm"	118
73.	Primitive Habitation	120
74.	Rocky Mountain and Brown County Roads	121
75.	Cartoon—Need of a Coliseum	123
76.	Welcome Home in 1916	126
77.	A "Homey" Old Country Place	127
78.	"The Big Woods" and "Little Hoosier Church"	128
79.	Newer Buildings of Indiana Colleges—	
	Notre Dame University	136
	Franklin College	136
	Indiana University	137
	Hanover College	138
	Butler College	138
	DePauw University	139
80.	Illustrations Showing Progress and Development in Various Fields—	
	M. Rumely Co., Laporte	140
	Studebaker, South Bend	141
	Eli Lilly & Co., Early Buildings	142
	Eli Lilly & Co., Recent Buildings	143
	Gary, Indiana. Steel Mills, New Theater, and Y. M. C. A. Building	144
	Indianapolis News Building	145
	Indianapolis Star Building	146
	Polk Sanitary Milk Co	147
	Nordyke & Marmon Co	148
	National Motor Vehicle Co	149
	Traction Terminal Building, Indianapolis	150
	Claypool Hotel, Indianapolis	151
	Washington Hotel, Indianapolis	152
	French Lick Hotel	153
	West Baden Hotel	153

TO ALL INDIANIANS, PRESENT AND ABSENT,
THIS VOLUME IS AFFECTIONATELY DEDICATED

Scope and Character of the Proposed Celebration

By the Committee.

The Centenary of Indiana's statehood is near at hand. Cognizance was taken of the approaching event by the Legislature of 1911 in the creation of a Centennial Commission to recommend a site and suggest plans for a permanent memorial. The action of the Commission in deciding upon a Library and Museum was universally applauded as wise and patriotic. That the succeeding Legislature will approve this movement, considering it with that largeness of view, consistent with the State's history, achievements and prospects, we take for granted. A splendid Library and Museum of the monumental design and fitting environment contemplated, will supply an urgent present need, typifying the patriotic and intelligent spirit of the Commonwealth today; and stand a hundred years hence to proclaim with dignity the high character of citizenship in 1916.

As stated in a succeeding chapter, on authority of the Indiana Centennial Commission, the law of 1911 did not empower them to go farther than recommend a site and prepare plans for a permanent memorial. Any consideration of a formal celebration was not contemplated in the act. Meantime there has arisen a spontaneous and wide-spread sentiment in favor of an adequate and appropriate celebration. In response to this feeling and upon call of the Governor and Indiana Centennial Commission there was held in Indianapolis, on May 3, 1912, a banquet at which the matter of a suitable Centennial Celebration was carefully considered. Various sections of the State were well represented by men of distinction, including Governor Marshall, Charles W. Fairbanks, members of the Indiana Centennial Commission, members of the House of Representatives, eminent jurists, educators, clergy, representatives of Indiana's leading business organizations, newspaper men, and public officials. The Hon. Chas. L. Jewett, Chairman of the Centennial Commission, presided. As expressing the enthusiastic sense of that meeting, the following resolutions were adopted:

1. That we commend the movement initiated and under the direction of the Indiana Centennial Commission, to establish a State Historical Library and Museum building, of ample size, artistic design,

(Loaned by H. J. Friedley)
First State House of Indiana, located at Corydon. In excellent state of preservation

and with proper setting for architectural effect, as a permanent memorial, to mark the end of the century of the State's existence.

2. That supplemental to the historical library and museum, we believe there should be a Centennial Celebration of such dignity and duration as to fittingly typify the State's history, achievements, growth, wealth and resources, and likewise set forth its possibilities; that the celebration in its essential features should be historical and educational in character, with commercial and trade features as secondary.

3. That in the consummation of such a celebration Indianapolis should set about to secure the erection of a splendid coliseum and music hall, the same in conjunction with the Historical Library and Museum, to house such historical, educational and other exhibits as may be developed and demonstrated by experts during the course of the celebration; that for one period of the celebration the coliseum should be used for a great farm machinery and automobile show; at another period, agricultural and horticultural products; for the third, a great Olympic; for the fourth, a great music fest in which trained bands, choruses, orchestras from the various cities of the State, after prolonged coördinated preparation, might be brought together in a great music festival, etc.

4. That in our judgment the work of the State Board of Education, the State Board of Agriculture, the State Board of Health, the State Board of Charities and the Indiana Historical Society should be coördinated and harmonized in any attempt at a celebration.

5. The foregoing plan of celebration in our judgment offers great advantages, amongst which may be enumerated:

(a) It is possible of accomplishment without great expense to the State.

(b) The historical exhibits which will be developed will be saved to the State and preserved in the archives of the new Museum for the instruction of present and future generations. Relics and documents of unpurchasable value will be saved which would otherwise drift to other States and be lost to us for all time to come.

(c) The plan of educational exhibits demonstrated by trained experts will offer to all our citizenship knowledge of real value which they may carry home and apply. These exhibits will reveal to the people the needs and possibilities of education, in all its phases; will show the unsuspected and undeveloped natural resources about us on every hand; will make plain the necessity of better conserving our natural resources, the soil, the forests, the mines, the purity and beauty

Second State House of Indiana, Indianapolis

of our streams, and above all teach the lessons relating to the conservation of human life and health.

The Indiana Centennial Celebration Committee was created as a result of the general meeting held on May 3d, and the resolutions just quoted have formed the basis for the recommendations which follow.

The succeeding chapters contain suggestive outlines for the Celebration prepared by persons especially competent to speak upon the subjects they treat. Their suggestions are earnestly commended for serious consideration by the General Assembly, as the wise and carefully-thought-out work of experts. Of the State's varied activities only a small part has received consideration. It is only offered as a tentative plan, to be elaborated and perfected by painstaking labor and thought during the three years to come.

With the event so near at hand it is well to take reckonings. In so important a matter it is the height of unwisdom to drift. Lagging will end in conventional mediocrity. Early attention will enable carefully wrought plans and ample time for their fulfillment.

An Educational and Historical Celebration as advised will or should require on the part of thousands of persons, the most painstaking preparation. It will mean intelligent and well manned central organization, in active touch with all the cultural and moral forces as well as the productive industries. Wise agitation and direction as well as efficient organization will be necessary in every county of the State.

This will require time. It will likewise take money; not an enormous sum and yet sufficient to insure a campaign of instructive planning in every community. A liberal fund should be available for the purchase of historical pictures, manuscripts, relics, specimens of fossils, minerals, or archæological remains for installation in the Museum; also for prizes to stimulate historical research in the schools and promote the preparation of community exhibits. Money invested in this manner will be of the greatest practical advantage, in promoting the educational phase of the Celebration, and bring to the Museum material of inestimable value.

As the year 1916 approaches there should be regional celebrations and "try-outs," preparing the way for the culminating event. The greatest benefit accruing to the State from such Historical and Educational Celebration will arise from the thorough course of training necessary to its successful achievement.

In considering the scope and character of any proposed celebration, the conventional exposition has not been deemed worthy of serious thought. Such are in their essential features great department store exhibits, entailing enormous expense in the construction of temporary buildings which serve the purpose of a day and are torn down; an unwarrantable extravagance. It is the prime purpose of this Committee to inaugurate and promote a method of commemoration which will not only be dignified and appropriate but give permanency of results to the entire citizenship. Our history, achievements and growth are inspirational. Why not let them speak to the world through the people who have wrought so well. Educational and Historical Exhibits, demonstrated by experts will insure the greatest good to the greatest number. They will give that breadth of knowledge which is an asset of value, power and permanence.

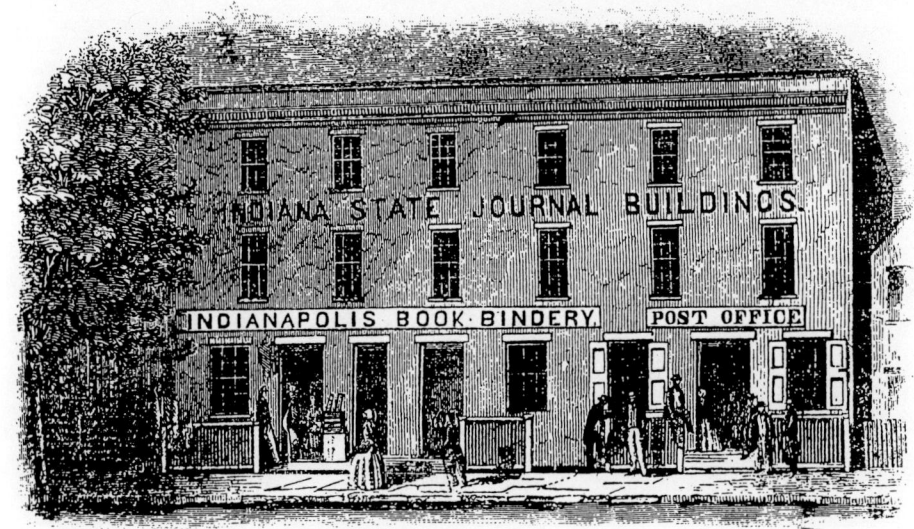

Post Office, Indianapolis, 1850

In the year 1908 the city of Quebec proclaimed in splendid pageantry to assembled guests from all the world, the story of her history. For a fortnight the citizens of New York City and every village upon the Hudson consecrated themselves to impressive and uplifting ceremonies in commemoration of the work of Hudson and Fulton. It is well that we celebrate each year with proud acclaim the birthday of the nation and of our illustrious national hero.

But what of Indiana? Has the Commonwealth an unworthy past? Was it a small matter to struggle with the privations of pioneer life, to brave the terrors of wild beasts and barbarous tribes? Is it of no moment that in all the national wars of the past century Indiana has played a noble part? Is it a trifling matter that in these hundred years endless forests and swamps have been supplanted by fertile fields and prosperous cities, with humming factories and busy commerce? Who can contemplate without swelling pride the transition from the log schoolhouse to our unexcelled public school system, the growth of our colleges and flowering out of the simplicity and culture of our Hoosier life a literature to which all the world pays homage. Once the term "Hoosier" implied opprobrium. Now the title is worn proudly, emblematic of character and worth.

Present Indianapolis Post Office Building

In the face of these facts what Indianian is so unresponsive to patriotic sentiment as to oppose a fitting celebration of Indiana's Centenary in 1916? We refuse to believe there are such.

The time and the occasion are not ordinary. The situation calls for the broadest coöperation and the most exalted patriotism. It demands the abolishment of political lines and sectional feeling. Let us recognize no north, nor south; no Evansville, no Fort Wayne, no Indianapolis; but only *Indiana*. Hoosierdom belongs to us all. Let us celebrate her Centenary worthily. Indiana is the geographical and cultural heart of the Nation. Let it throb with patriotism in 1916!

The Indiana Centennial Commission

Demarchus Brown.

The Indiana Centennial Commission was created by the law of 1911 for the purpose of selecting a site and preparing plans for the memorial building to commemorate in 1916 the admission of Indiana

The Great Question

Where to put 'Em?

into the Union. The law defines the purpose of this building to be the "proper housing of the State Library and Museum, Public Library Commission, and the educational and scientific offices of the State." This memorial shall be known as the "Indiana Educational Building."

Present State House of Indiana.

The third to be erected in seventy-five years. Entirely inadequate. Officers cramped for room. Valuable historical relics, specimens, books and records driven to corridors or into dingy and damp basement rooms, where they are not available or suffer decay

The Centennial Commission consists of Colonel Charles L. Jewett of New Albany, Senator Frank M. Kistler of Logansport, Representative Joseph M. Cravens of Madison, Hon. Charles W. Fairbanks of Indianapolis, and State Librarian Demarchus C. Brown. This Commission under the law is concerned only with the plans and the erection of a suitable memorial building. The members are alive, however, to the importance of a proper celebration of the State's Centennial apart from the dedication of the proposed structure.

There should be a historical pageant which would bring before the eye of the people the development and growth of Indiana. There should be exhibitions in agriculture, manufacturing, education, art, transportation, music, and all departments of life. These will be made as permanent as possible because the celebration must be far removed from the ephemeral exposition. A worthy celebration carried out in a dignified manner will not only be instructive but a source of inspiration for the future.

While not authorized by the statute to do so, the Centennial Commission called a meeting of public-spirited citizens in May, 1912, to discuss the whole question. The meeting was representative of the entire State and showed great interest in the celebration of the centennial of Indiana's admission into the Union. An organization was formed to arouse public sentiment on the subject and to keep the matter before the people. It is hoped that this organization will be strengthened and supported by the Centennial Commission, even if an enlargement of the powers of the latter should become necessary for that purpose.

The Centennial Commission desires not only the collection and preservation of the State's history and relics of all kinds in a great library and museum which shall be a useful institution to all the people, but it hopes to see a universal interest in the history and development of the commonwealth and a profound concern for its past. Indiana has not done what other States have in the preservation of its history. Can the public be aroused to a fuller appreciation of this matter?

A great celebration at the time of the dedication of the memorial building in 1916 will do more to awaken and keep alive the public interest than anything else. This means if the celebration be done in a worthy, dignified way, and if the building be a beautiful and useful monument. This is what the Centennial Commission is planning, and what it will recommend to the Legislature.

Growth and Achievements of the Law

Addison C. Harris.

The beginning, growth and achievements of the law in Indiana make an interesting chapter in the history of our State. This history begins with the capture of Post Vincennes, on February 25, 1779, by General George Rogers Clark. He was a commissioned officer in the military service of the State of Virginia, commissioned by Patrick Henry, as Governor; and so by the rules of international law, the land he took by his conquest, being all the territory northwest of the River Ohio, became the property of the State of Virginia. There being white inhabitants at Post Vincennes and at a few other points in the territory, it became the duty of the State of Virginia to establish a government for their protection. To this end, the House of Burgesses of Virginia shortly after the conquest created all the land northwest of the river Ohio into a distinct county, and the Governor appointed a county lieutenant with authority to organize and maintain a proper force for the maintenance of peace and order, who at the same time established a court of civil and criminal jurisdiction at Post Vincennes composed of several magistrates. Colonel J. M. P. Legreas was made president of the court, which court sat from time to time, and some of its decisions were taken on appeal to the court of last resort in Virginia.

After the victory at Yorktown, in the treaty of peace between the United States and Great Britain, made on our part by Benjamin Franklin, John Adams, John Jay and Henry Laurens at Paris on November 30, 1782, this land northwest of the river Ohio was treated as being a part of the State of Virginia. But it was the general sentiment of all the people at that time that inasmuch as all Americans had been engaged in the common cause against Great Britain, that in equity and good conscience, the fruits of Clark's conquest should belong to the United States itself. The statesmen and people of Virginia acknowledged the justness of this claim. And so on December 20, 1783, the Legislature of Virginia, by an act, directed the representatives of that State in the Congress by proper deed to cede all this land to the United States, and the deed was signed, acknowledged, executed and delivered on the first day of March, 1784, by Thomas Jefferson, Arthur Lee, James Monroe, and Samuel Hardy, then delegates in the Congress from the Commonwealth of Virginia. And thus

Government House, of the Territory of Indiana, Vincennes. Still in excellent state of preservation

this land became the property and passed under the jurisdiction of the Federal Government.

On July 13, 1787, the Congress passed an act, commonly known as the Ordinance of 1787, for the government of the territory of the United States northwest of the river Ohio. This ordinance declared among other things that slavery should never exist on this soil and that the inhabitants should be entitled to the benefits of jury trial, proportionate representation in the Legislature, and that "religion, morality and knowledge being necessary to good government and the

Governor Jennings, the first Governor of Indiana

happiness of mankind, schools and the means of education shall forever be encouraged." It was also declared in the ordinance that the territory should as the population increased be in time divided into five States and admitted into the Union on an equal footing with the original thirteen States in all respects whatever, and each State when created should be at liberty to form a permanent constitution and State government, and secure to the people of the several States the fundamental rights of liberty, religion and education, pledged in the ordinance. On May 7, 1800, all that part of the land lying west of the now

Tippecanoe Battle-ground, near Lafayette

State of Ohio was by Congress constituted a separate territory under the name of the Indiana Territory. A territorial government was organized on July 4 of that year. General William Henry Harrison was appointed Governor. The seat of the territorial government was fixed at Saint Vincennes, and a territorial legislature and a territorial court were at once organized. The house in which the legislature and court sat is still in existence in Vincennes. In the year 1813 the seat of the territorial government was removed to Corydon.

On April 19, 1816, the Congress passed an act to enable the people of Indiana Territory to form a constitution and State government, and for admission into the Union, and authorized the election by the people, of representatives or delegates to meet at Corydon and then form a constitution and State government, and declaring that when formed such government shall be republican and not repugnant to the fundamental articles of the Ordinance of 1787. A constitutional convention accordingly met on June 10, 1816, at Corydon and adopted and established a State constitution and form of government. Jonathan Jennings was president of the convention and the first Governor of Indiana. The Supreme Court assembled at Corydon on May 5, 1817. Shortly afterwards Governor Jennings appointed Isaac Blackford to the supreme bench, which position he held as the leading member of that tribunal for more than thirty-five years, and until by the adoption of the present constitution of the State (which was but a series of amendments to the old constitution of 1816) the Supreme Court judges ceased to be appointive and became elective. More than fifty judges have sat upon the supreme bench of the State during its first century, and many are known throughout the Nation for their learning and ability. The court from the beginning had official reporters, among which may be mentioned Albert G. Porter, Benjamin Harrison and John W. Kern. The rights of the State were represented in this great court by attorney-generals, among which may be mentioned Joseph E. McDonald, Oscar B. Hord, and William A. Ketcham. The first Legislature after the adoption of the present constitution contained many of the leading lawyers of that period. They revised and reënacted the laws of the State. They abolished the old forms of practice in the courts, and adopted the simpler methods provided by the code which was in fact written by Lucien P. Barbour, a leading member of the Indiana bar.

Another great reform enacted by that Legislature was the statute greatly enlarging the rights of married women, which measure was championed by Richard D. Owen.

A few years ago a great step was taken in the administration of criminal law by the adoption of the indeterminate sentence of criminals to prison.

It is not necessary to name the many forward steps made by the Legislature and the courts of this State throughout the past century towards the better form of government. This would require a full chapter in the history of the State.

It is believed that the growth and development of the legislative and judicial departments of the State government could be shown by gathering together in a museum or department the portraits of the great men of the early times engaged in laying the foundations of our State government, among which may be mentioned General George Rogers Clark, Thomas Jefferson, Governor Jennings, and others; and portraits of all the judges of the Supreme Court, headed by Judge Blackford, together with the reporters and attorney-generals of the State and men who have distinguished themselves in the Legislature from year to year in the enactment of good laws. There to be gathered together, also pictures of the first assembly building as it still exists in Vincennes; the State House at Corydon, with the historic elm under which the constitutional convention sat; the first court house in Indianapolis in which the Supreme Court also sat after the removal of the capitol to this city and before the completion of the old State House; the first State House and Supreme Court building in this city occupied for twenty years and the new State House in which the Legislature and courts now sit; together with pictures of the county court houses of the early period, followed by a display of the court houses in the several counties of the State at the present time. In such museum would also be accumulated many historical documents connected with the history of the State, letters, autographs and portraits of the judges and others, including those of lawyers who, assisting in the administration of justice, elevated and made the bar of Indiana equal to that of any other State in the Union.

Religion

Francis H. Gavisk and M. L. Haines.

The coming State Centennial should give an opportunity for presentations of the history of the religious life of the people of Indiana of special interest and value.

Religion in its various forms of manifestation has been the power more potent than any other to mould and inspire the lives of our citizens to higher issues.

Little Cedar Baptist Church, near Brookville, Indiana.

Begun in 1810, completed in 1812. The earthquake of 1811 came near to causing abandonment of the undertaking. After long fasting and prayer, work was resumed and the building completed in 1812

The record of the progress of the various churches and religious societies of the commonwealth could be set forth in a series of charts and pictures, each denomination furnishing its own.

Along with these there should be provided in a loan exhibition such historical mementoes—portraits, books, relics—as would be vivid reminders of the religious life of past years.

A number of the events of importance in the history of the churches could be set forth in historical pageants and tableaux in a

McKendrie M. E. Church, near Brookville

manner similar to that in which the work of world missions has been presented by the churches in London, Boston and Cincinnati.

Illustrated lectures and addresses on the early struggles and various lines of advance of the different religious denominations should have a place on the program.

The story of the coming of the heroic Catholic priests and of the devoted Protestant missionaries to the Indian tribes of our territory; the struggles of the scattered pioneer churches in the new settlements; the experiences of "circuit rider" days; the coming of the Friends to eastern Indiana and what that settlement has meant to the upbuilding of the State, these and many other forms of religious and church life, potent in their influences, should be presented.

There should be included also in these exhibits the institutions, educational and philanthropic, that have come directly out of the religious life of the people.

This means that the private schools and seminaries, and the colleges founded and maintained by the religious denominations should be classified with the churches as expressions of their life.

So the hospitals, and orphanages, and "homes," and other institutons for the sick and the needy, should not be left out when the works of mercy which religion has wrought are presented.

This is but a brief outline of what should be done. When the character of the observances of that celebration are more definitely determined upon then plans that will fit in with all the other exhibits can be presented more fully in regard to the religious exhibits and observances.

"Circle Hall," Indianapolis. Distinguished because at one time it was Henry Ward Beecher's church

St. Mary's Catholic Church, Indianapolis

Indiana History and Its Celebration

James A. Woodburn.

The Indiana Centennial should keep in view two aspects in commemoration of Indiana history.

I. It should be the occasion and the means of promoting the study, collection and preservation of materials for the history of Indiana.

II. It should produce a worthy public celebration and commemoration of the historic past of the State.

The first of these ends will relate to what is of the more permanent and enduring value, the latter to the more immediate, popular, and spectacular side of the centennial celebration. Let us speak first of the second aspect of the centennial year.

I.

While a material and spectacular celebration of a hundred years of the State's history will be fleeting and will pass away with the jubilee exercises of the year, yet its influence may be abiding for years to come. This aspect of the celebration is of importance, and much care and attention may wisely be devoted to it. It may be made an expression of noble devotion to the State, of a worthy public spirit and a fine patriotism which may beget in the rising generation a deeper love for Indiana, and a more intelligent appreciation of her achievements, while to the generation that is passing from the stage of action there may be given much joy and satisfaction in having been a part of a worthy past.

Let us portray in pageantry a hundred years of Indiana history before the people of the State. This can be done by

(A) A grand spectacular procession through the streets of the capital city, illustrating many interesting and varied aspects of our history. We would suggest a visual illustration and a representation, by means of *floats* or a *series of tableaux*, of the following:

I. Pioneer Life.
   1. An Indian Group,
      The Wigwam, showing the industry and domestic life of the Indians. The descendants of Indiana Indians may be obtained.

2. The Life of the Pioneer Trapper and Wood Ranger, the *Coureurs de Bois*.
3. La Salle and the Jesuits.
4. The Pioneer Settlement at Ft. Vincennes and Ft. Wayne, and Ouiatanon; The Trading Post.
5. The Scene of the Transfer from the French to the English.
6. George Rogers Clark and the Capture of Vincennes, 1779.
7. Tippecanoe.
8. The Inauguration of the Territorial Government, 1805.
9. The Council of Gen. Harrison with the Indians.

II. THE PERIOD OF SETTLEMENT.
1. The early Log Cabin: Half-Faced Camp.
2. Early Log Cabin: The Round Log Type.
3. Early Log Cabin: Hewed Log Type—Interior view, woman spinning, etc.
4. Making the Constitution under the Corydon Elm.
5. Gov. Jennings taking the Oath of Office.
6. Making the New Purchase, 1818.
7. The Founding of Indianapolis.
8. Transfer of the Capital to Indianapolis: How Samuel Merrill Transported the Treasury.
9. An Early Church Meeting.
10. The Circuit Rider.
11. An Early Schoolhouse. Scenes from the Hoosier Schoolmaster.
12. The Founding of Indiana University.
13. Early Transportation and Travel.
    (a) The Pack-horse.
    (b) The Ox Team.
    (c) Coaching and Post Days.
    (d) Flatboat and Canal Boat.
    (e) The Early Tavern.
    (f) The "Movers" and the Conestoga Wagon. Scenes on the National Road, of which Washington Street was a part.
    (g) The Early Steam Train.
14. A Political Campaign. "Tippecanoe and Tyler Too." Log Cabin and Hard Cider, and the Coonskin.
15. A Husking Bee and an Apple Peeling.

The Pioneer Type of Hoosier Residence

The More Pretentious Type of Residence, found through Southern Indiana in the '40s and '50s

III. SLAVERY AND THE WAR.
1. The Underground Railway.
2. Lincoln Speaking at Indianapolis *en route* to Washington.
3. Gov. Morton offering Troops to Lincoln for the Union.
4. Gov. Morton Commissioning Union Officers, Lew Wallace, et al.
5. Union Soldiers Leaving for the Front.
6. The Women at Home in War Times.
7. Arrival of News from the Front.
8. The Boys Coming Back from the War.
9. Indiana's Record in the Civil War; Roster—Number Enlisted, Dead, Wounded, etc. Tableaux of Arms.

IV. LATER INDUSTRIAL AND MATERIAL DEVELOPMENT.
1. Mining.
2. Agriculture.
3. Manufacturing.
4. Transportation.

V. A SERIES OF TABLEAUX, SETTING FORTH THE LIFE OF THE STATE IN
(a) Literature.
(b) Art.
(c) Science.
(d) Education.
(e) Human Welfare.

These are tentative suggestions.

Other features will be thought of and the details and the execution of the spectacle can be wrought out by care and thought on the part of those who are competent and skilled in the art of exhibition.

(B) In addition to the spectacular procession we could have a play, or a series of tableaux in a fixed place with repeated performances during the centennial celebration. They should be designed to illustrate scenes, incidents, and characters in Indiana life. Men like Mr. McCutcheon could supply a series of popular cartoons to picture to us the past, and, no doubt, men of the standing of Mr. Meredith Nicholson, Mr. Booth Tarkington, Mr. Charles Major, and Mr. George Ade, would lend their literary and dramatic art to promote a suitable memorial celebration in honor of the State. The best mind and talent of Indiana can be brought to the service of such a worthy enterprise. A good basis for such a dramatic presentation might be found in Mr. McKnight's work, "Indiana, A Drama of Progress."

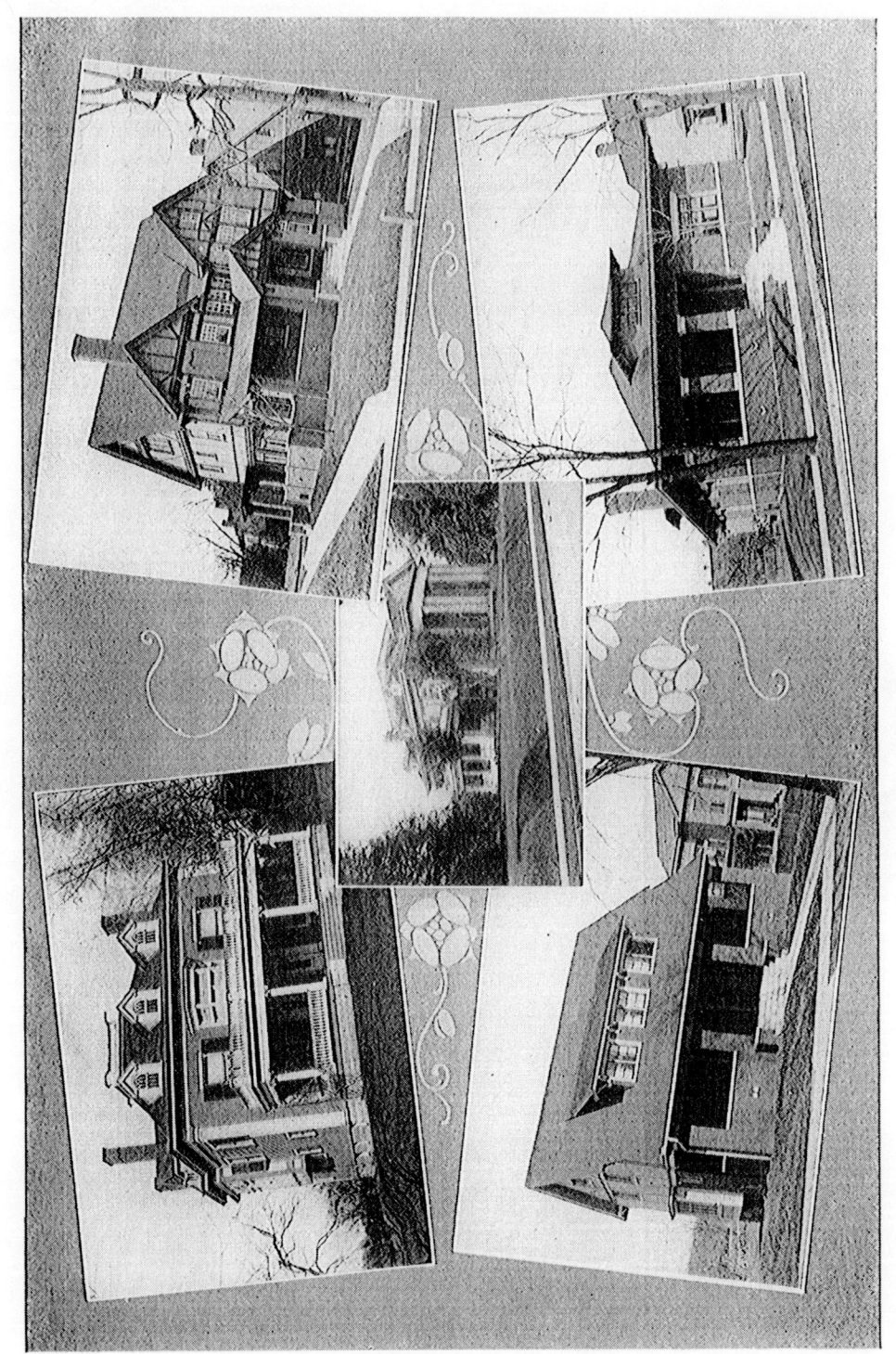

Group of Modern Residences, Crawfordsville, Indiana

II.

But what we do for Indiana history should not pass with the day or the year of the celebration. The centennial should produce a more abiding result. It must leave us richer in historical materials, in the sources from which the history of the State may be written, and in creditable accounts of that history. The occasion should lead the State to do more for the preservation of materials for her history, and to promote the collection, editing, and publication of materials that will have a value to the State for the centuries to come. The State should make suitable provisions for fostering *an Indiana Historical Survey*, such as is already begun in Indiana University. The survey should keep in view certain definite ends:

1. The preparation and publication of a *complete bibliography* of *Indiana History*.

This should present a list with a brief description, of every known work—book, essay, pamphlet, etc.—touching any period or phase of Indiana history, with a citation as to where the work may be found. This should be supplied to every library in the State so that any citizen of the State who wishes to know may easily learn what books and sources are available in print on the history of the State.

2. There should be organized and directed effort for the *collection, preservation,* and *publication* of *Indiana historical material*. There should be a well-sustained agency constantly at work for the attainment of this end.

The materials that are being wasted and lost should be saved and collected, placed in the proper libraries for safe keeping, catalogued and arranged for the use of students and writers. Pamphlets, books, letters, documents, newspaper files, journals of travel, diaries, etc., all such materials should be saved from being lost or destroyed or carried away from the State. Indiana, from lack of provision and of proper public concern, has been remiss in this respect in the past. The people of the State should be encouraged to save these materials of their history and to place them where they can be safe-guarded and be made most easily available for use.

3. In the third place the State should encourage and sustain the publication of a *series of monographs* on Indiana history. Such monographs might not be profitable in the book-trade, though they may be of the highest value. They should show the result of a careful and scientific study of our history. They can be undertaken and worthily produced only by men or women who have been suitably trained for such work or who have a faculty for historical research.

Maps prepared by Ernest V. Shockley, under the direction of the Department of History and Political Science of Indiana University

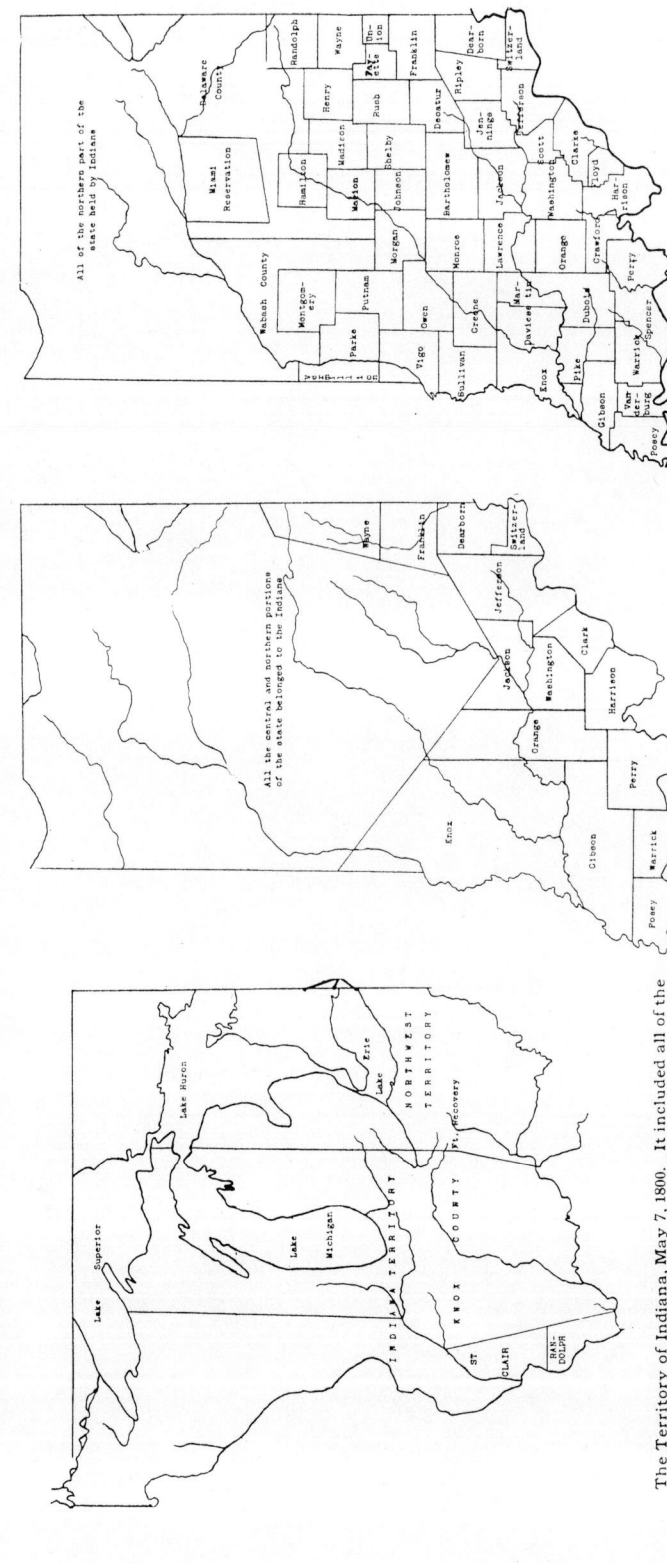

The Territory of Indiana, May 7, 1800. It included all of the Northwest Territory west of a line drawn from the mouth of the Kentucky River to Fort Recovery, thence due north to the northern boundary of the United States

Map of Indiana at the time of admission in 1816

Map of Indiana in 1824 when the capital was moved to Indianapolis

Their real value will be in exact proportion as they are the products of serious, scholarly, painstaking, and scientific study. No commercial enterprise will produce the results desired. The centennial year will likely bring forth for sale to the public a batch of mushroom writings called *Histories of Indiana*. They will generally be the products of a few months or of a single season's hurried work, based on inadequate materials, and generally prepared by persons who have few qualifications for writing history. Such publications will add nothing to our real knowledge of the history of the State. Their prime purpose will be to make money for their publishers and authors. Many of them will be carelessly prepared, erroneous and misleading, dealing with unauthentic and fanciful stories and exaggerated myths. To counteract such misinformed and misinforming work, it seems eminently desirable that the State should undertake the publication of a series of historical collections, comparable to those of Massachusetts, New York, Michigan, etc., and such as Illinois is now carrying out in a notable way. If the centennial can bring to pass such a desirable and lasting result, it will be a cause for praise and gratitude by the generations that are to come.

Literature

MEREDITH NICHOLSON.

I have been asked to give an opinion as to the best manner in which the literary achievements of Indiana might be recognized in the proposed centennial celebration. In such a matter many views

Edward Eggleston, Author of the Hoosier Schoolmaster

are possible, and it should be understood that I make these suggestions only because they have been asked through the courtesy of the committee having the plans in preparation, and with no feeling that they are final at any point.

House in which Edward Eggleston was born, Vevay, Indiana

Lew Wallace

Author of Ben Hur

It occurs to me that a pageant would make possible an expression of the life and growth of the State that would speak at once for the pictorial arts, for the drama, and for literature as well; and that, wisely conceived and generously executed, such an item of the program would make a very wide appeal. In England the pageant has in recent years been carried far and with distinguished success; and only last summer, in Detroit, an historical pageant was presented that attracted many thousands of visitors to that city. The successful pageant is not turned out lightly in a day, but requires long and intelligent study; like an egg it must be good or it is bad; there is no middle ground; and a good pageant costs money. There are in the universities and colleges of Indiana men and women quite capable of putting through a pageant of the first order. Miss Charity Dye, for many years in the English Department of Shortridge High School, at Indianapolis, arranged a number of successful pageants, I believe, and she possesses a great deal of information on the subject, both historical and practical. I should think it would be wholly possible to arrange a single pageant, or a succession of pageants, expressive of Hoosier progress, with the aid of the teaching staffs of the colleges; and the students of our colleges and high schools would be obviously the material from which to draw the active participants. Probably in no other way could so many lines be brought together and harmonized—educational, historical, literary and artistic.

At the time the proposed State Library and Museum is opened it would be well to set apart a division for the preservation of Indiana literature. The present library has no such department. Recent Indiana fiction is placed in circulation for the use of employes of the State House and many of the books are badly worn. There is no space in the present library for the maintenance of an Indiana division; but in my judgment all the books of Indiana writers that have any value, particularly those that are interpretative in any degree of the Hoosier people, should be carefully preserved. It can not be pretended that every book written by an Indianian is entitled to such a place. There has been a disposition to claim as Indiana writers men like Joaquin Miller and the late John Hay who, while born within the State's borders, and writers we should be proud to include in our pantheon, were never in any way identified with the State. The line must be drawn somewhere, and both judgment and courage are required in establishing it. No one could be better qualified than the present State Librarian for this task. In these days the lives of many books, even of very meritorious ones, are brief. It is exceedingly difficult to ob-

Mr. Wm. Young reading to Gen. Wallace for the first time his dramatization of Ben Hur

Gen. Lew Wallace's Study, Crawfordsville, Indiana

tain copies of books that are not yet ten years old, in their original forms; and the Department of Hoosier Writers should have first editions as far as possible. These volumes should be for display and for reference; and once carefully begun the department should be maintained through the years.

It would, I think, be an interesting feature of the proposed exercises of the centennial celebration to exhibit this department, and to have in connection with the opening an address by some one who would deal sympathetically but critically with Indiana's contributions to the national literature. The speaker should be chosen with care, and the occasion might best be served by the choice of some one not identified with the State in any way.

I take it that the Library and Museum will become in time the recipient of tablets, busts, and other memorials, commemorative of Indiana's eminent citizens in every department of life; and very likely, with proper attention, some such memorial of one of our greater Hoosier writers might be in readiness for the centennial. This should be clearly a representation of some writer of indubitable standing, and I suggest Edward Eggleston, James Whitcomb Riley, General Lew Wallace and Maurice Thompson as men whose recognition has been so general that the State would honor herself in honoring them. In the case of Mr. Riley, it would undoubtedly be very easy to raise, by private subscription, a fund sufficient to procure a bust or bas relief, and I should like to see the dedication of such a permanent tribute to his genius made a feature of the exercises.

In connection with the maintenance of an Indiana division in the new library, I suggest that there might be gathered also for the centennial and as the nucleus of a permanent collection, autographs and manuscripts of some of the Indiana writers. The MS. of General Wallace's "Ben Hur" is, I believe, preserved intact; and doubtless some of the MSS. of Maurice Thompson, Dr. Eggleston and Mr. Riley could be obtained.

Elementary Education

Charles A. Greathouse.

The public school system of Indiana has had an interesting and decided development, especially in the last fifty years.

The spirit of the cause of education was not absent even in the territorial organization, for we find in the Ordinance of 1787 that, "religion, morality, and knowledge being necessary to good government and the happiness of mankind, schools and the means of educa-

First log schoolhouse in Wayne County, 1813. Also picture of Jonathan Roberts, who attended school in this building in 1814

tion shall be forever encouraged," but although this idea was brought out again and again and emphasized under the constitution of 1816, the school system was merely upon the statute books, and for thirty-five years or more little was accomplished but "confusion and ruin."

School legislation under the constitution of 1851 was an early consideration, and in 1852 and 1873 definite and permanent steps were taken toward the establishment of free public schools, and today Indiana ranks second to no State in the Union in her system of common schools.

In the working out of this public school system many important factors and lines of study have developed that are possible of material representation for the purpose of a centennial observance.

The school building in its evolution from the little one-room log schoolhouse to the capacious modern edifice may be shown by actual buildings in miniature and by pictures.

School furniture and general equipment in their marvelous development, from the wooden bench and rough table to the up-to-date steel furniture and adjustable seats with convenient and sanitary desks, may be made an instructive collection. Here, too, will appear the old water-bucket and common gourd or dipper by the side of the automatic sanitary drinking fountains of today, while globes, maps, charts, and numerous other helpful devices may be added.

An interior of the old log building with its bare walls, puncheon floors, poor light and ventilation may be shown in contrast to the

The little red school building was the successor of the log schoolhouse.
Picture of the schoolhouse at Kyle, Indiana

beautiful, well-lighted, heated and ventilated modern building, with its pictures, statuary, plants, and many other attractive and useful features.

The old primer with its simple rhymes and crude pictures will find a place near the pictures cards, letter cards, number cards, carefully planned charts, and other materials for the primary instruction of today.

Text-books in all subjects may be obtained and a valuable exhibit made that will show the great improvement not only in subject-matter, but in kind and character of books. The changes in paper, print, illustrations and titles will be apparent.

Modifications in ideas and methods of discipline will be in evidence, where the ferule, emphasizing the "don't" side of discipline is in strange contrast to the modern basement playrooms, materials for games, playground apparatus, and gymnasiums.

Recent type of county school building, Leroy School, Winfield Township, Lake County

Hobart Township Consolidated High School, Lake County

The old stove, roasting the pupils seated near it and allowing those farther away to freeze, may be displayed with the modern heating and ventilating plants meeting all the sanitary requirements of evenly distributed heat and pure air.

The transportation wagon, a symbol of the consolidated school, can be shown.

Schoolroom interiors of manual training and domestic science departments may be fashioned, and the objects made in these departments in the schools shown, while by pictures or otherwise corn club contests, poultry and horse judging contests and other agricultural study may be represented.

Pictures can be procured not only illustrative of many lines of development, but to show the individuals who have been most active, in times past and present, in shaping the affairs of the school.

In collecting, selecting, and arranging these materials, no doubt, other schemes for showing the growth of the common schools in Indiana will suggest themselves.

Of course the facts of school legislation, the accreditment of training schools for teachers, the classification of high schools, the origin and maintenance of young people's and teachers' reading circles and countless other valuable educational movements in the State cannot be shown in any objective way.

The First Buildings of

Wabash College
North Western University, now Butler College

Earlham College
Franklin College

Hanover College
University of Notre Dame

Collegiate Education in Indiana

Wm. Lowe Bryan.

I. Books.
1. Books and other publications giving contributions of Indiana college and university men of learning.
2. Books and other publications giving contributions of Indiana college and university men to general literature.
3. Books, bulletins, catalogues, etc., about the Indiana colleges and universities.

II. Charts.
1. Charts showing the development of the curricula of studies in Indiana colleges and universities, including all professional schools. The curriculum is the constitution of a college.
2. Charts showing from what States and countries and from what educational institutions the members of the faculties of Indiana colleges and universities have come. These will show from what sources our educational influences have come at different periods of our educational history.
3. Charts and maps showing the distribution of our college and university alumni within the State and throughout the country and the world. These will show the range of influence in our educational institutions.
4. Charts showing the occupations of alumni at different periods of our history. These will show the influence of our educational institutions upon economic and social life.
5. Charts showing enrollment at different periods and the increasing ratio of college enrollment to population. Few social facts are more significant than this increasing ratio.

First Building of Indiana University

III. PICTURES.
1. Persons: Loan exhibit of portraits of eminent professors, with large print cards giving brief biographies.
2. Buildings:
    (a) Pictures of early buildings.
    (b) Pictures of present buildings and interiors.
3. Equipment:
    a and b as for buildings.
    In this connection also an exhibit of apparatus.

First Buildings of Asbury University, now DePauw

IV. LECTURES.

A series of lectures adequately illustrated by means of apparatus and pictures, including moving pictures, setting forth in an attractive way the most important advances in learning between 1816 and 1916. In most fields of learning the advances within that time have been of enormous importance. They could be so presented as to be intensely interesting. Suppose, for example, an address showing by a few striking examples the state of our knowledge in physics in 1816 and then illustrations of the three or four greatest discoveries since that time. It is true that an indefinitely large series of lectures could be made in this way, but also the right men could pick out a few typical things to say and to show. This series could be made one of the most attractive features of the entire celebration.

V. STUDENT ACTIVITIES.

If it is thought best, the student activities can be shown in such a way as to add greatly to the entertainment features of the celebration. For example:
1. College plays: Greek, Latin, French, German, Classic. English, Modern.
2. Music, Operas, Choruses, Glee Clubs, etc.
3. Athletic Games.
4. Other Student Clubs and Organizations such as Y. M. C. A.

Music

EDWARD B. BIRGE.

Indiana has kept abreast of her sister States in music during the 100 years of her history, the musical foundations laid in the early days having been followed by a remarkable development of choral and instrumental concerts and festivals, while the public high schools and the elementary schools have made very notable progress along these lines during the last twenty-five years. This rapidly increasing musical activity has not been confined to any one section of Indiana, but is State wide, as is evidenced by the numerous annual music festivals held in widely separated districts of the commonwealth.

"On the Banks of the Wabash Far Away," by Paul Dressler

The proposed centennial celebration of 1916 should recognize to the fullest extent and in as striking a way as possible each of the broad lines of musical activity already mentioned. The most obvious way of doing this would be to organize a great music fest to occupy several days. This festival should bring together in fullest coöperation the leaders in music, the singers and instrumentalists of the State.

There should be an impressively grand choral concert, combining the best singers (to the number of about 1,000) of all the music festival societies of the State, and also an orchestral and artist concert of equal significance along the same coöperative and representative lines. One entire concert should be devoted to public school music.

There should also be given opportunity for an address dealing with the history of music in the State of Indiana during the last one hundred years.

As the great underlying purpose of the centennial is an educational awakening throughout the State as to our power to do things now and also in the future, no time should be lost in so shaping the musical affairs in the different sections of the State that from now on all musical activities will be a forecast of the culminating events of the year 1916.

The first step toward this end should be a preliminary campaign of education in every district as to the purposes and aims of the centennial and an urgent invitation should be given every district to

The Noblesville Band, 1850. Led by R. L. Carlin, still living and active at 81

cultivate its musical activities to the utmost with the idea of having representation in the final celebration. As a result of this preliminary campaign musical festivals should spring up in districts where heretofore such festivals have not been held, and the artistic standards of the existing festivals should by the same means be greatly raised.

As the time of the centennial year begins to draw nearer (some time during the year 1914), plans should be made to have the centennial music the chief object of musical interest during the year preceding the centennial, and the music should be studied and produced on as large a scale as possible by the musical forces of each district.

Finally, after this preliminary waking up, each accredited body of singers and instrumentalists should be invited to send representatives to take part in the final culminating event.

To this great musical fest should be invited the famous singers and other prominent musicians who are native Hoosiers, but who are living in other parts of the country.

To sum up, we should—

First, have an educational campaign to awaken interest and arouse ambition.

Second, have all musical activities henceforth contributory to the centennial idea.

Third, have the centennial music studied and performed by all the various musical bodies of the State.

Fourth, a great representative body of musicians from all parts of the State perform the centennial program.

Art

Frederic Allen Whiting.

If the history of art and its relations to the development of the industries of the State, as well as to its general culture, is to be adequately represented at the coming centennial celebration no time should be lost in completing the preliminary plans. The proposed State Museum would seem to furnish the natural housing for such an exhibition, and it should be definitely planned for this end, and the ex-

The Herron Art Institute, Indianapolis

hibits gathered for the purpose of installing a permanent chronological exhibit. Such an exhibit should include examples which would show the range of work produced by each of the painters, sculptors and other artists who have, since its settlement, done their part in giving the State a very definite heritage and tradition in art matters. These works of art should be so arranged as to show the development of art in the State, and should form part of the permanent collection of the museum. If for the time of the centennial celebration other exhibits overcrowded the new museum I am sure that the Art Association of Indianapolis, Indiana, can be counted upon for the heartiest coöperation. In such an event the chronological exhibit of paintings, etc., might well be temporarily installed at the John Herron Art Institute.

Such an art exhibit should be based on a thorough study of the history of the State, and include examples of the handicraft of the red men who inhabited the territory formerly. For example, many fine pieces of "Stone Age" craftsmanship have been found within the present borders of the State.

It would be well to have the preparation of these art exhibits considered in relation to the industries current at the time of their

Exhibition of Art Work in Richmond

production and to show the part which art has always played in the development of industries; to show also the evolution of such present industries as the automobile, from the bicycle, buggy, etc.

The building should, of course, be of appropriate character, dignified and monumental, and built so far as possible of material procured within the State and by our best artisans. It should represent in itself a monument of the best building our own people can produce after 100 years of statehood guided by the Hoosier spirit.

In the building should be some central rotunda or other important architectural feature which might well be enriched with mural deco-

Exhibition of Art Work by Students in Indiana Schools

rations by our best local painters. Such men as Steele, Forsyth, Bundy, Stark, Adams and Wheeler, for instance, would undoubtedly enter with enthusiasm into the spirit of such an undertaking, putting their best effort into the work, which could be done in such a way as to cost a very small amount, while adding a local and appropriate beauty to the building.

I would also suggest that arrangements be made with some able artist, as Mr. George Grey Barnard, one of the most virile and original of American sculptors (and having intimate associations with Indiana through the fact that his mother and father are residents of Madison and his sister of Indianapolis), to produce for some appropriate setting at the entrance of the building or within it, a splendid figure or group to represent, in durable stone or marble, his interpretation of that Hoosier spirit which has given the State its high position and enviable reputation. Another artist who might well be asked to take part in the enrichment of the building is Miss Janet Scudder, a sculptor of splendid achievement, who was born and reared in Terre Haute, Indiana.

These are only tentative suggestions. It is a long task for an able committee to work out the details so that when the building is ready there will be assembled for installation an exhibit which shall visibly and adequately represent to the people of today the past which has alone made the advantages of the present possible.

Central Engineering Building, Purdue University

Outline for An Exhibit of Technical Education

WINTHROP E. STONE.

Indiana's achievements in technical education will constitute an interesting and attractive feature of its centennial celebration, particularly in connection with the historical and educational exhibits of the State's industrial development.

Indiana ranks ninth among the States of the Union in manufacturing and its institutions for technical education stand among the first in their efficiency. While this phase of education did not exist in the earliest days of the State and its development has come wholly in the last fifty years, it has become an important factor in the State's progress and would from its very nature claim a large share in any historical summing up of Indiana's development.

For the purposes of the contemplated exhibit, this subject would be presented under the following heads:

(a) Exhibits of illustrative material such as photographs, charts, etc., depicting the buildings, laboratories and classes of the institutions engaged in this field.

(b) Exhibits of apparatus, models, machines, drawings, and products used in connection with or resulting from technical instruction.

(c) Exhibits showing actual operations in the laboratories, shops, and classrooms of technical schools.

(d) Exhibits of the literature of technical education, text-books, manuals, and publications representing the contributions of teachers and investigators in the field of technology.

The State has within its borders two prominent institutions devoted to technical education, viz., Purdue University and Rose Polytechnic Institute. Besides these, other higher institutions would contribute from some departments related to technology. The leading manual training schools at Indianapolis, Richmond, Fort Wayne, Evansville, and elsewhere would show what is being done in secondary education in this field. Doubtless also some of our manufacturing plants could contribute exhibits illustrating their plans for teaching employes for special industrial operations. The Y. M. C. A. classes and night schools would also be expected to furnish some material of this kind.

Agricultural Experiment Station, Purdue University

The whole exhibit of technical education might be classified under the following groups, in each of which there would be an abundance of material of popular and educational interest:

1. Exhibits illustrating technological education in its stricter sense.

a. Instruction in shop practice, including pattern making, molding, and casting, forging and machine shop practice.

b. Instruction in mechanical drawing and descriptive geometry

c. Instruction in civil engineering, including surveying, railway location, municipal engineering (including water supply, sewage disposal, etc.), masonry and frame structures, bridge design, materials testing, hydraulics, road-building, etc.

d. Instruction in mechanical engineering, including machine design, generation and transmission of power, steam engineering, railway mechanical engineering, gas engineering, heating and ventilation.

e. Instruction in electrical engineering, including engineering design, generation and transmission of electrical power, electrical measurements, electrical railway, telephone, and illuminating engineering.

f. Instruction in chemical engineering, including technical and manufacturing chemistry, synthetic and analytic manufacturing processes, electro-chemistry, metallurgy, etc.

g. Instruction in the sciences fundamental to engineering and technology, viz., chemistry, physics, biology, mathematics, etc.

2. Exhibits illustrating industrial training, instruction in trade schools, special schools, etc.

a. Special methods, processes, and classes in connection with any given industry.

b. Y. M. C. A. and night classes.

3. Instruction in connection with transportation. Devices and methods for instruction in railway operations, signaling, air brake, mechanism, etc.

Technical education more than any other lends itself to exhibition methods on account of dealing with tangible things, materials, products, and processes and this department of the State's centennial exhibit will, it is believed, be of more than usual interest. An important feature would be the actual operations of laboratories with students and instructors in attendance, testing machinery, conducting experiments, making drawings, and blueprints, using instruments of precision, etc., etc., in almost unlimited variety.

The Purdue Herd

Agriculture

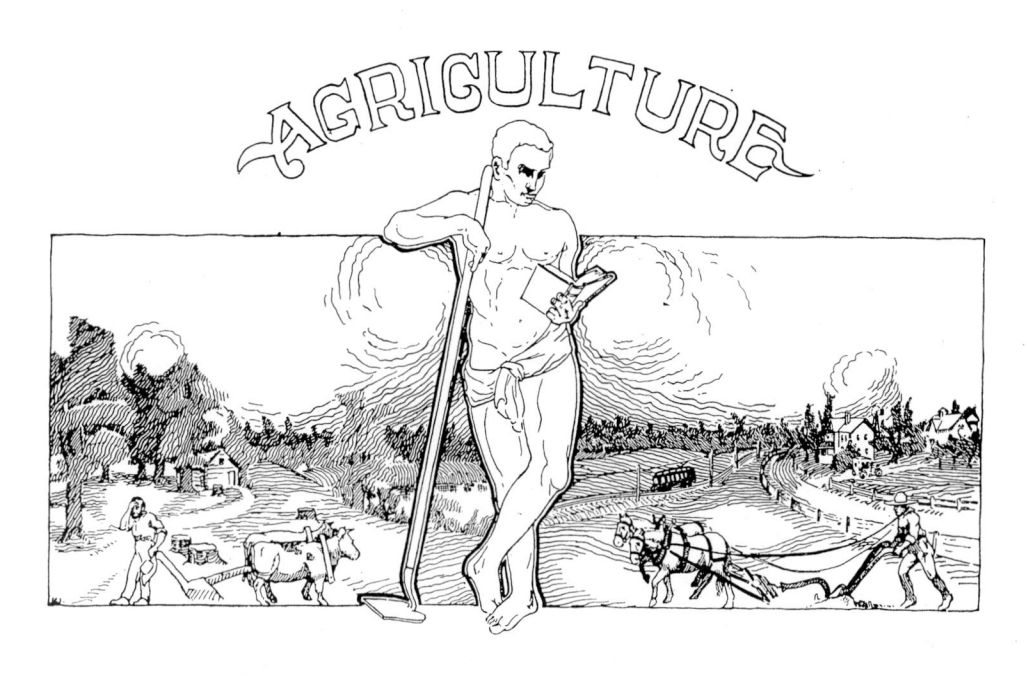

G. I. Christie.

Indiana agriculture should occupy a prominent place in the centennial celebration exercises of 1916. While this industry has been the basis of the progress and the prosperity of Indiana from the beginning, it is found that agriculture is being recognized more and more by all classes of people. A few of the factors which have brought this condition about are:

1. The rapidly increasing value of land.
2. The extremely high cost of food stuffs.
3. The movement of young people from the country to the city.
4. Soil robbing and other wasteful practices resulting in reduced crops.
5. New ideals in education and revised courses for rural schools.
6. The discovery and popularizing of facts which mean better and larger crops and a more economical use of same.

In the presentation of the subject, attention should be given to the historical, experimental and educational phases of the work. By means of graphic illustrations, moving pictures, lectures and demonstrations, everyone, both young and old, should be made to realize the magnitude of agriculture and its development from the earliest days to the present and the future possibilities.

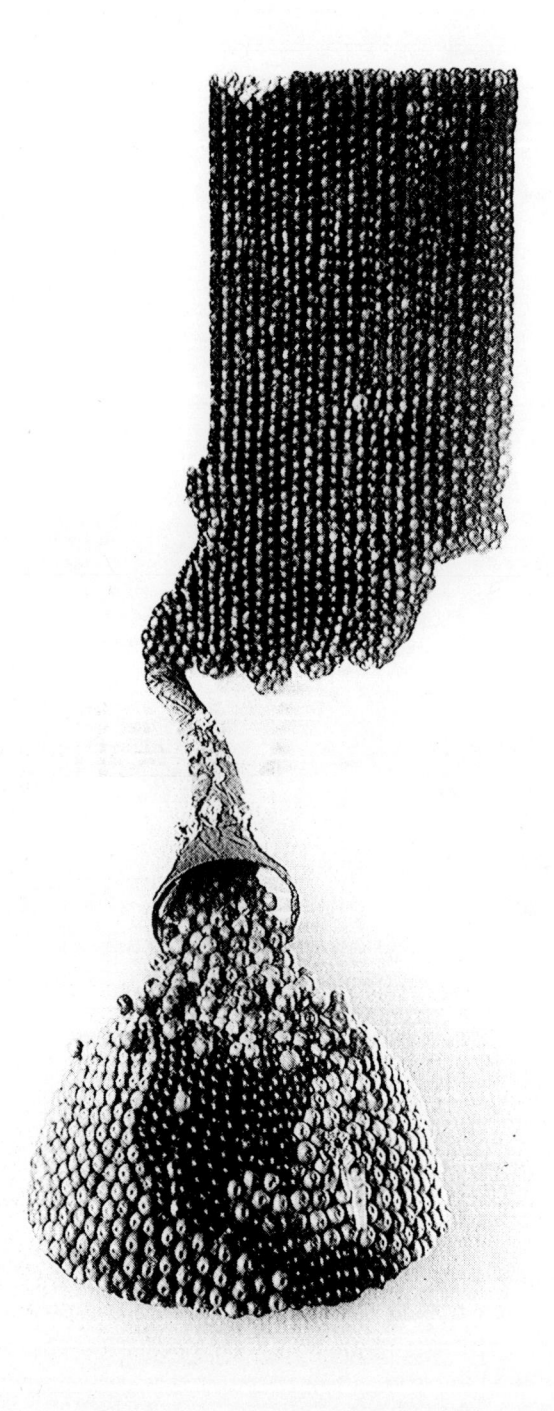

What Indiana might do in Apple Production
—A. W. Brayton, Jr., and A. W. Lockhart

Soil.—A graphic presentation of the condition of the land of Indiana at the different stages of development during the century; a comparison of the implements used in tilling the soil, seeding the various crops, harvesting and threshing; common methods practiced in depleting soil fertility compared with more modern scientific soil management.

Crops.—A presentation of the extent and variety of crops grown in the early days and methods of handling and utilizing the same, compared with those of one-hundred years later.

Live Stock.—This branch furnishes most interesting and valuable material for exhibits and demonstrations. Kinds of live stock, methods of rearing and feeding, marketing and utilization in the early days, compared with the changed conditions of the present.

Dairying.—With the increase in population has come an increased demand for dairy products and corresponding changes in the methods employed one-hundred years ago with those of today and a presentation of the various steps taken in the development.

Horticulture.—Fruit growing has occupied an important place in Indiana agriculture from the first. The extent and development of the fruit belt, varieties, cultivation, methods employed in production, marketing, etc.

Educational Agencies.—In the early days of Indiana agriculture, farmers gained their information largely from the field of hard, and many times, costly experience. Today, they are given an opportunity to learn and benefit by the experience of others and to gain information from scientific research. To portray the steps of development along these lines will be of great interest and value.

The State School of Agriculture.—A presentation of the work at different stages in its development and the methods employed in instruction.

The State Experiment Station.—A display of the work of this institution covering twenty-five years; the results of many discoveries relating to farm problems and the extensive system employed to reach and assist all farmers.

The Extension Department.—Demonstrations in the use of the educational train; the farmers' movable school; the farmers' institute; contests; the county and State fair exhibits and other methods employed now as compared with the old methods of projecting information or reaching the farmer in his home.

The Rural School.—The development of the course of study and the place agriculture occupies in the rural school instruction, compared with that of the early days.

Giant White Oak. A lone monarch of Indiana's primeval forests

Forestry

Stanley Coulter.

In any observation of the admission of Indiana to the Union, forestry should have an adequate representation. The relation of forestry to progress of the State has been and is so evident as to need no argument. There should be exhibited in an educative and striking way—

First. What we originally had.
Second. What we now have.
Third. What we might have.

Without going into specific details, under the first head should be shown maps showing the distribution of the original forests of the State, the density of the stand, composition of the stand, size of individual trees, etc.

The progressive clearing of the land for agricultural purposes. This would make a desirable series representing the condition of the forests by decades.

The distribution of this material including the log house, the rail fence, log roll, the rise and fall of wood-working industries.

A collection of the important economic woods of the State together with photographs of the typical species. "Cut" of Indiana forests for successive decades.

Under the second head there should be shown maps giving the distribution of the present forests, the density and composition of the stand, the average size of the individual trees.

The distinction between wood lots and wood pastures should be demonstrated with a series of illustrations representing good and bad conditions. The highway and street trees should also be presented in this connection showing their scantness in number, their poor selection, their defective spacing, lack of protection, bad treatment, etc.

Under the third head methods for reënforcing existing stands, the formation of new plantations, cleanings and thinnings, protection against fire, insects, fungous diseases, etc., selection of species for reënforcing, for forming new forests and for streets and highways.

This, in a very broad statement, indicates what the purpose should be. Details could be extended almost indefinitely and we are convinced that a definite treatment under the three main heads indicated at first would be not only highly attractive but also of educational value.

A Rocky Mountain Forest. Rugged and beautiful, but monotonous in the sameness of the trees. Compare this with

An Indiana Woods. Note the variety of foliage and charming artistic beauty

Public Health

J. N. Hurty.

To help forward the public health cause the Indiana Centennial Celebration would offer many excellent opportunities. That the public health needs to be bettered appears when we remember our sick rate is at least 50 per cent. higher than it should be, and lowers the public efficiency to an equal degree.

To this subnormal efficiency, due to preventable sickness, may in great degree be ascribed the reason why that in the last fifty years there has not been an increase in the acreage yield of our farming lands. Much sickness is not conducive to productiveness.

HEALTH EXHIBITS.

In the centennial celebration, public health exhibits could be made which would exercise a powerful influence for strengthening of the people. By succinct and lucid tables, by graphic charts, drawings and pictures, could be shown the present birth, death and sickness rates, and by comparison with the normal rates or rates of other peoples, we could be made to appreciate our position and thus excite efforts for betterment. An exhibit could be arranged to illustrate plainly what the *science of hygiene* actually is and what it can do to increase strength, wealth and happiness. Münsterburg has said "hygiene can prevent more crime than any law," and this certainly being true, the people would learn from the hygiene exhibit that sole reliance should not rest upon the law and the courts to prevent crime. They would also learn that "health is wealth" and also the greatest source of happiness.

Preventable Diseases, from whence they come and how they may be prevented, would occupy a good proportion of the exhibit. The importance of preventing preventable diseases appears when it is known that they kill 1,000 persons monthly in Indiana and cause 10,000 cases of sickness. The annual cost to the people of the State is fully $15,000,000. Even the most uninformed could imagine an exhibit showing the loss in money, lives and strength, from diphtheria annually. This would be followed by charts, diagrams, pictures and mottoes clearly illustrating from whence the terror comes and how it can be prevented. The same could be done with scarlet fever, typhoid fever, infantile paralysis, pneumonia, consumption and the whole list of preventable diseases.

PURER STREAMS.—The streams are not for the purpose of being made into sewers. They are intended to carry health, beauty and refreshment throughout the land. In many instances the people of Indiana seem to have believed streams were made to be polluted. It is highly essential to our future welfare that the streams should be kept pure and reclaimed where they have been abused.

It would be important, therefore, to exhibit maps of the streams and water sources of the State, show charts of surveys of the same,

Indiana Tuberculosis Hospital, Rockville

give their sanitary condition, give analyses and statistics as to sewage and industrial wastes cast into them.

Also, to show by photographs the beauty and material wealth of pure streams and the ugliness and harm done by pollution.

Such an exhibit could not fail to pay its costs many times in wholesome and much needed lessons to us all. The sanitary surveys already made by the State Board of Health of the west fork of White River, of the Wabash River, and of the Ohio River, would, if publicly presented in exhibit as above set forth, be of inestimable value to our State.

HYGIENE OF MUNICIPALITIES.—Indiana municipalities need to learn much more of the profits to be derived from hygiene. An exhibit of hygienic and unhygienic conditions of cities and towns would be most profitable and calculated to arouse interest in good municipal housekeeping. To have our municipal hygienic faults, which result in great losses, made clear to us, could not help but start us on the way to health betterment in cities and towns.

To make an exhibit at once instructive and stimulating, tables of statistics of the death and sick rates of cities could be prepared; these

Sanitary survey should be made of many beautiful
Indiana streams for the purpose of protecting
and keeping them pure, as a source of
water supply for the people

figures could be made plain by diagrammatic and graphic charts; photographs of good and bad conditions would be placed side by side for their contrast effect, illustrations and descriptions of sewers and sewage disposal with cost and statistics of efficiency, also full information of water supplies and water works could be presented. Paving, parks, public playgrounds and all municipal undertakings for the betterment of living could be illustrated and otherwise exhibited.

SCHOOL HYGIENE.—There is no more important governmental matter needing attention than school hygiene. Raise the children in physical health and the matter of intellectual and moral development will in large degree be solved. Realizing this fact our State has enacted school hygiene laws and under them within two years, new sanitary school houses exceeding three and a half million dollars in value have been built. This great advance in the care of our children could be illustrated most advantageously in a centennial exhibit.

A school hygiene exhibit would consist of models and pictures of sanitary school houses; models and illustrations of ventilation and warming methods; plans and pictures of sewage disposal, of water supplies, of sanitary drinking fountains, of sanitary clothes lockers, of sanitary furniture and adjustable desks, of baths, playgrounds and of sanitary methods of sweeping and cleaning.

LECTURES AND PAMPHLETS.—Facilities for giving illustrated lectures, would, of course, be provided. These lectures would cover all phases of hygiene and teaching of public health and preventive medicine. Such lectures, illustrated with still slides and moving pictures would not only instruct but would also greatly entertain all visitors. The celebration and the exhibits would furnish excellent opportunities to distribute health pamphlets to visitors and thus further spread the gospel of good health.

FINALLY.—I am heartily and enthusiastically in favor of having a *centennial celebration*. It could not fail of instructing the people in ways patriotic and material, in arousing a deeper patriotism and furthering a higher citizenship, in supplying a wholesome and needed public entertainment and establish a monument marking progress and achievements in the first hundred years of our State's existence.

Outline for Proposed Athletic Events

T. F. MORAN AND HUGH NICOL.

In connection with the various historical and educational exhibits with which it is proposed to celebrate the one-hundredth anniversary of the admission of the State of Indiana to the Union, it will be important to present the development of those legitimate means of recreation and amusement which have found favor with the people of the State. Prominent among these will be athletic sports and contests.

While the development of athletics in the modern sense is coincident with the last decades of the century, it must not be overlooked that the early pioneers and settlers had many unique and interesting forms of athletic sports. To revive these and present them at the celebration will be of more than usual interest to our citizens. The implements of sport, the games themselves, and all that will bring to the minds of our present day citizens these old-time sports and contests will be both recreative and educational as well as having important historical bearing. It is proposed, therefore, to secure all possible information as to these old-time games and provide ways and means for their actual projection before the spectators at the time of the celebration.

Another phase of the same subject will be to arrange for a series of athletic exhibits and contests exemplifying the most modern development in this field and in which Indiana men and institutions have achieved no small reputation.

Public Swimming Pool, Recreation Department, Indianapolis Health Board.   Average daily attendance 500

There should be, perhaps, some attention given to professional sport as the development in professional baseball games, but for the most part these contests should be in accordance with amateur standards and rules.

We should have a variety of classes, in some of which the higher institutions of learning would participate, in others the secondary schools, in others organizations and institutions such as the Young Men's Christian Associations, in others amateur clubs and teams representing communities or organizations such as the Turnverein, athletic clubs, etc.

Public Play Ground, Recreation Department, Indianapolis Health Board

While to the student these exhibits would present much of interest, at the same time, they would serve for those recreational features which form so important a part of any public exposition.

These games might extend over a considerable portion of the summer season or a week or two might be set aside during which time these would form distinctive features of the celebration. Following is an outline of athletic contests which are suggested. Some of these contests to be restricted to certain classes of athletes, others to be open to all. In connection with these games prominent "old athletes" who have achieved fame in the athletic world, might be called upon to act as officials and thus bring an added interest to the assemblage.

1. State ''Olympic'' meet for high school athletes, with teams organized by counties.
2. State baseball tournament for high school teams.
3. Track and field meet for colleges and universities.
4. College baseball tournament.
5. Open meet for all amateurs.
6. Gymnastic meet for colleges.
7. Open gymnastic meet, turners, etc.
8. Open obstacle race.
9. Cross country race, open to all amateurs.
10. Water sports—if possible.
11. Wrestling for college teams.
12. Wrestling open to amateurs.
13. Tug of war—colleges vs. athletic clubs.
14. Bulldog tug.
15. Open tennis tournament.
16. Fencing contests.

Civic Co-ordination and Park Development

Henry Jameson.

The last decade has seen a tremendous impulse toward the better arrangement of cities. Prior to that time, outside a few of the great Eastern cities, little or nothing had been accomplished in the way of bringing into systematic relationship those physical features of a city that are now recognized as constituting the inseparable parts of a city's park system, using that term in the broad sense that includes civic centers and all other nuclei of community activity. By this is meant such things as the great avenues and highways of a city, its parks, open spaces and playgrounds, and the streams and bodies of water lying in and contiguous to it.

There is now an awakening in all of the larger cities to the vital importance of what we term park development, and under this particular head comes, as suggested before, that part of a city's building which pertains to its better arrangement and coördination, and not merely to the acquisition of parks.

From an economic standpoint, there has heretofore been in our American cities tremendous waste of energy on account of the lack of facilities for direct and convenient intercourse and traffic between the various sections of a city that must be reached in the daily life of the people.

This spirit of better growth should receive prominent attention at the forthcoming historical and educational celebration of the State's centennial. The movement for better parks and playgrounds, coupled with the conservation of streams and water fronts in our cities, should be given the impulse and stimulation essential to its further development by bringing it clearly and emphatically before the greatest possible number of people. This, it would seem, might be accomplished in many ways at an educational exhibition of this character.

One of the methods which might be most effective in showing the progress toward city planning in Indiana would be an exhibition of photographs or pictures illustrating the contrast between conditions before improvement took place, and after changes were made under the direction of competent landscape architects and engineers. Inasmuch as no great community work may be carried forward without the knowledge and intelligent coöperation of the great majority of taxpayers, the various things to be accomplished by better planning,

Beautiful Streams like this are found in the vicinity of every town and city in Indiana. Keep them pure and beautiful for the health and enjoyment of the people and by the establishment of playgrounds and parks and protected streams, should be as lucidly set forth as possible. To this end, there should be relief maps on a large scale, illustrating not only the æsthetic, but the economic effects, in a physical way, of such development.

To stimulate a widespread interest, that would be far-reaching in its effect, competitive prizes might be offered to the various cities of the different classes for the best plans offered for civic development, playgrounds, parks and stream conservation. This should not only

Old Wooden Bridge, common in the earlier history of the State

create a healthful rivalry, but should go far to bring about an awakening of the people of the various cities to the fact that such intelligent and systematic development is just as essential and possible in the smaller as in the larger cities.

In connection with such an exhibition, there might be shown models of the various playground developments, with demonstrations of what may be done in playground instruction. This would be an extremely essential feature, as showing the educational character and value of a complete scheme of park development.

At frequent intervals during the period of the exhibition, illustrated lectures might be given by men prominent in this field of human endeavor. These should touch all the various phases of the work—its effect upon the citizens and its absolute necessity, not only from an economic, but also from an æsthetic point of view, helping the masses to recognize the intrinsic value of the things in our everyday life that are fine and beautiful, and which are more essential to the humbler citizen than they are to his wealthy and more prominent neighbor.

New Bridge, of Indiana stone and concrete, not only artistic but built to stand until the next centennial celebration in 2016

There are so many different avenues and channels through which, by an exhibition of this character, the people could be stimulated and brought to realize the necessity of better environment, particularly in our cities, that it could be made one of the most important features of such a splendid enterprise as is proposed for our centennial celebration. Finally, emphasis should be laid on the fact that the factor of quality should come to be the great essential in our city growth and should dominate the spirit of progress hereafter, rather than, as has too often been the case heretofore, the idea of quantity.

Showing conditions before treatment by a City Park Board

Same locality as preceding, after clearing of "dumps" and park development

Proposed Plaza to the west of the State House in which it was suggested that Indiana, Indianapolis and Marion County should bear a proportionate expense, to the end that the splendid Capitol Building should be protected from objectionable environmental structures, and ample ground be provided for future extension of the State's buildings

Charities and Correction

Amos W. Butler.

How many know the extent of Indiana's public charitable and correctional agencies? In the year 1910-11 the State and its subdivisions expended through all their official charities, including the expense of truants, $3,681,279.27. The number of persons cared for or aided was 83,871.

The Early Type of Indiana Jail

Public responsibility for the poor and needy was first recognized in Indiana by the territorial law of 1790, which provided for relief of the poor by township overseers and justices of the peace. This was modified by the act of 1795, which provided also for the establishment of workhouses for such poor persons as were able to labor. These laws were the beginning of our system of outdoor poor relief. In 1852 the township trustees were made ex-officio overseers of the poor.

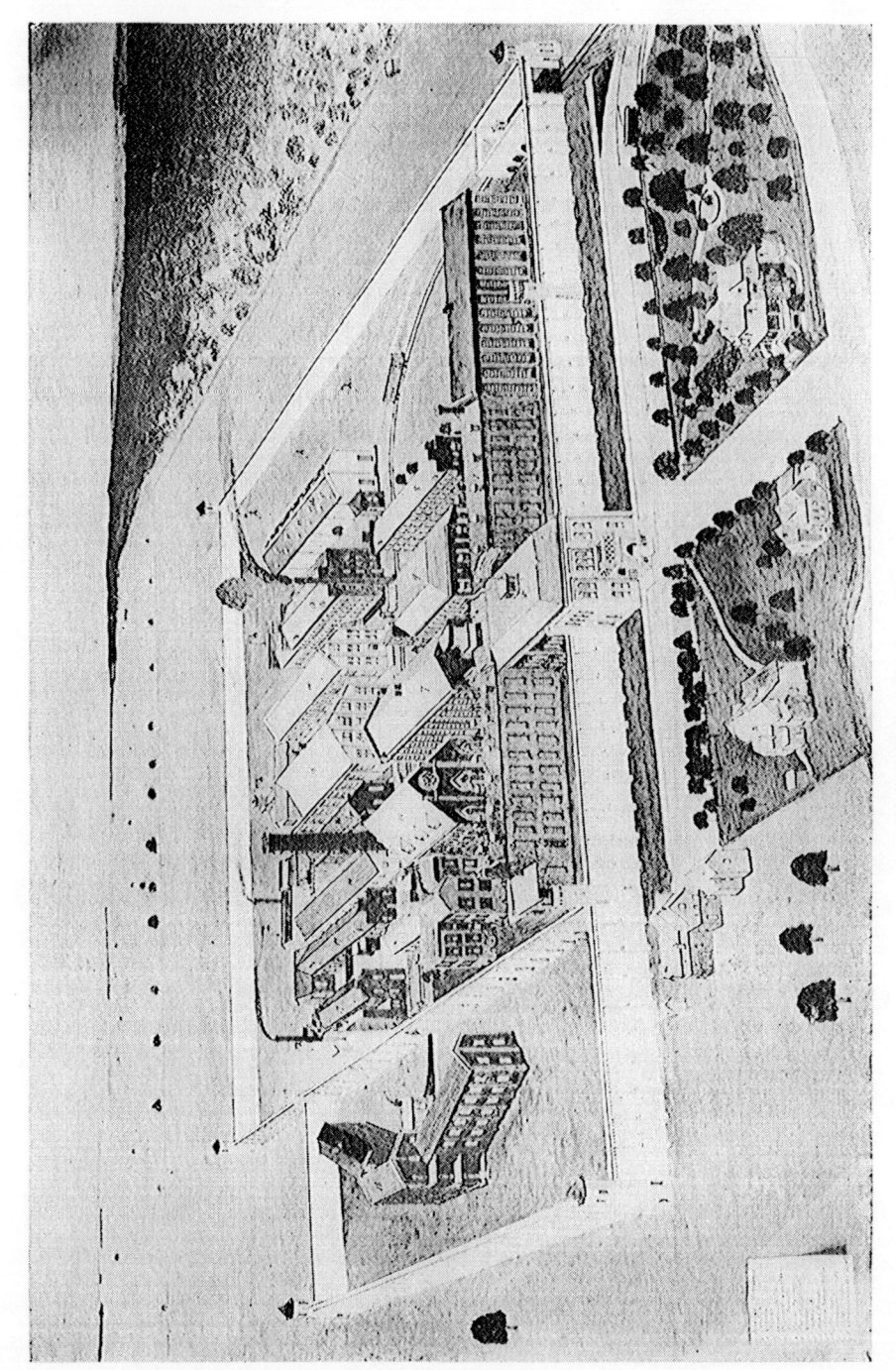

State Prison, Michigan City

In 1895 was the beginning of State supervision. That year the township overseers of the poor spent $630,168.79 for relief. In 1911 the expenditures for the same purpose were $271,078.64. The average expenditure from 1907 to 1911, inclusive, was $259,912.41 per year. State supervision had brought about an average annual reduction of $348,893 below the poor relief of 1895. In 1897 there were 82,235 persons aided from public funds; in 1911, 42,993.

The first law regarding dependent children was passed in 1795. This and one passed in 1821 provided for binding out such children. In 1895 authority was given boards of county commissioners to subsidize private orphanages and in 1881 they were authorized to establish orphan asylums. In 1889 boards of children's guardians were created and further extended in 1901. By the law of 1897 dependent children were made wards of the State and placed under State supervision. At the present time there are in effect and active operation laws prohibiting the retention of children between the ages of three and seventeen in county poor asylums longer than sixty days (1897 and 1901); regulating the importation of dependent children from other States (1899); requiring the approval of the Board of State Charities before any child-caring institution or association can be incorporated (1903); providing for the punishment of parents or guardians who wilfully neglect their children or allow them to become dependent (1907); making the juvenile court the only agency through which a child can become a public ward (1907); and lastly, the annual licensing of all child-caring agencies, public and private, including maternity hospitals, by the Board of State Charities (1909).

In 1821 was the first attempt to provide a poor asylum as authorized in 1816. The first county asylum was established in Knox County.

The first State institution was the Indiana State School for the Deaf, founded in 1844. Next came the State School for the Blind, 1847; then the Central Hospital for the Insane, 1848; the Soldiers' and Sailors' Orphans' Home, 1867; the School for Feeble-Minded Youth, 1879; the Northern Hospital for Insane, 1888; the Eastern and Southern Hospitals for the Insane, 1890; the State Soldiers' Home, 1896; the Village for Epileptics, 1907; the Southeastern Hospital for Insane, 1910; the Hospital for the Treatment of Tuberculosis, 1911.

In her penal and correctional institutions Indiana has made progress, though the greater part of it has been brought about since 1897. In the early days the guardhouses in the forts were used as

Old Orange County Infirmary

New Orange County Infirmary

places of detention. In 1792 the Legislature directed the establishment of jails, pillories, stocks and whipping posts, all to be under the charge of the sheriffs in the different counties. With two exceptions, each county in the State has a jail. The other forms of punishment were abandoned years ago. The first State prison was established at Jeffersonville in 1821; the one at Michigan City in 1860. In 1868 the House of Refuge, now the Indiana Boys' School, was opened at Plainfield; in 1873, the Indiana Reformatory Institution for Women and Girls, at Indianapolis. In 1907 the last named institution was divided. The girls were transferred to new quarters at Clermont, called the Indiana Girls' School; the old institution was called the Woman's Prison, and in 1907 there was added to it a correctional department for convicted women who would otherwise have had to serve their sentences in the county jails. Both the Woman's Prison and the Girls' School are managed solely by women. In 1897 the prison at Jeffersonville became the Indiana Reformatory, that at Michigan City the Indiana State Prison.

There are now seventeen State charitable and correctional institutions. On September 30, 1912, they had 12,448 inmates enrolled and an actual population of 11,410. For the fiscal year 1911-12, they cost the State $2,463,032.53. This was 40.7 per cent. of the State expenditure for all purposes, which amounted to $6,048,127.07. Measured by the good they do for unfortunate humanity and for the protection of society, and by their expense, they are the State's most important agencies, possibly excepting its schools.

It is nearly one hundred years since our forefathers decreed that the penal code of Indiana should be founded upon the principle of reformation and not of vindictive justice but it is only recently that we have interpreted this into law. The keynote of recent legislation has been prevention and reformation rather than punishment. Briefly it includes the indeterminate sentence and parole law of 1897; the jail matron law of 1901; juvenile court law of 1903; contributory delinquency law of 1905; adult probation and sterilization laws of 1907; county jail supervision law of 1909.

All these charitable and correctional agencies are under the supervision of the Board of State Charities, created by the Legislature of 1889. Its purpose is the supervision of the whole system of public charities of the State; its duty, to see that every inmate of every public institution receives proper care; that the public funds are properly expended; that the institutions are properly conducted and their management protected from unjust criticism.

Administration Building, Northern Hospital for Insane

A very interesting and comprehensive exhibit could be made of the charities or philanthropic activities of Indiana. This would illustrate the beginning and history, showing the development and expansion of all the charitable and correctional activities. It would include charts, laws, statistics, general information, concerning all phases of public charities, from the overseer of the poor and the first county jail to the most recent methods of the treatment of pauperism, the institutions for the care of the insane and feeble-minded, the modern conception of a State prison and reformatory. In all this work Indiana has had a conspicuous place and the people of the State can point with pride to the evolution of its institutions, to what has been accomplished and to the position they now hold. These exhibits could also include all forms of private or voluntary charitable activity, such as the work of hospitals, orphan asylums, homes for the aged, associated charities, children's aid societies. It would also include all forms of preventive work, including the work of the Red Cross, anti-tuberculosis, fresh air and pure milk campaigns, the problems of housing, child labor and playgrounds. All these agencies could be illustrated by photographs of buildings, grounds, equipment, occupation, recreation and amusements. There could further be an exhibit of the plan and scope of the work of each institution, together with copies of blanks and forms used. There could also be a large exhibit showing the result of the activities of the institutions and agencies, the work in the schools, the product of the shops, the output of the manufactories and all means and appliances used in the education, treatment, training, employment and diversions of both State and private institutions. In addition to this there could be a library made up of the reports and publications of the different institutions and organizations, and also a selected library of standard works on each subject illustrated by the exhibit.

Suggestions for the Display of Indiana Minerals, Fossils, Quarries, Mines, Etc., at the 1916 Celebration

David Worth Dennis.

STONE QUARRIES.—Every species of stone quarried in the State should be represented in the exhibit by one unfinished large block, and specimens of every tint or quality which the quarry offers for sale. Finished material of whatever sort should also be exhibited: fountains, columns, capitals, etc. Labels on cards large enough to be easily

An Indiana Quarry. The stone of Indiana quarries is more generally used throughout the United States in the erection of public buildings and other large structures, than that of any other State

read from the aisles should accompany each and every exhibit. These should give the commercial name, the chemical analysis if available, the mineralogical name, the geological formation and locality of each exhibit. A map of Indiana locating Indianapolis and the line or lines by which shipment of the stone may be made to various parts should be added. A large geological map of the State, unencumbered by unessential details, should go with the entire exhibit. Photographs should accompany the exhibit showing the mode of quarrying and handling the stone, until it is on the cars ready for shipment. Photographs of exposed bluffs of the stone will show its weathering qualities. In the case of building stone, photographs of the finished buildings should accompany the exhibits, together with the date of building the same.

Our most valuable building stone quarries are in the subcarboniferous limestone; striking geological and mineralogical phenomena accompany this limestone everywhere.

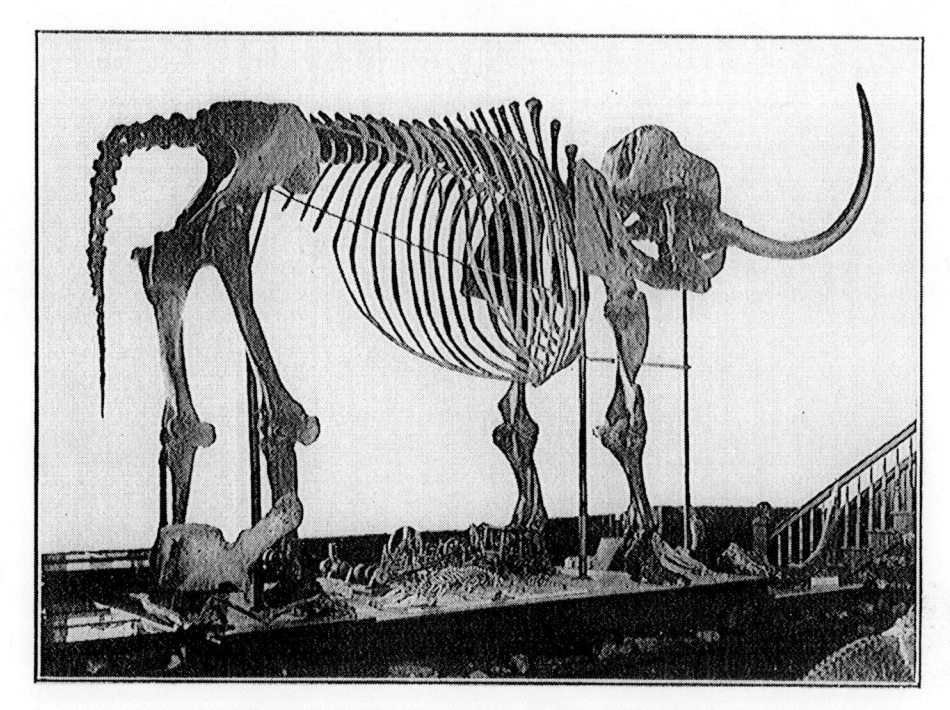

Skeleton of a Mastodon, Earlham College Museum

1. CAVES.—Wyandotte, Marengo and other caves should be fully illustrated with photographs. The largest stalactitic column in the world is in Wyandotte Cave, 100 feet in circumference and 175 feet high, on its lower side; the formation was able to grow a foot in 160 years. The label should ask how old is the cave? Marengo, though smaller, is more beautiful.

2. Sink holes are cave accompaniments. Thousands of them occur in southern Indiana. Some of these are dry, others are lakes or ponds. These should be photographed.

3. Lost River is the best key to the origin of caves. Photograph it.

4. THE SCENIC.—The Shades of Death, Devil's Den, Turkey Run, Rocky Hollow, Potrock Hollow, The Narrows of Sugar Creek, etc., between Bloomingdale and Crawfordsville, are extraordinary examples of erosion and should be photographed. They belong to the sub-carboniferous group. Some of the cave mouths are very striking and beautiful as well as instructive.

OIL FIELDS.—These should be represented by crude and refined products, maps, statistics, etc.

NATURAL GAS.—This should have historic notice in the mineralogical sections.

A Charming Ravine at "The Shades"   One of the Bluffs in the Gorge at "The Shades"

MINERAL SPRINGS.—These are susceptible of notice by samples of water and mineral deposits, etc. Photographs of resorts. Lodi springs have considerable sulphur deposits.

COAL MINES.—These should be represented as under stone quarries. Blocks, maps, labels giving heat units, analyses, extent and thickness of strata, and output.

CLAY.—Exhibits of the varieties, uses, wares, tiles, bricks, including of course kaolin and china.

GRINDSTONES AND WHETSTONES.—Same treatment. It is probably known to few Indianians even that the finest quarries for these purposes are to be found here that the world affords.

LIMESTONE FOR LIME AND LIME KILNS.—Same treatment. Processes, labels, statistics, growth of industry.

GRAVEL AND SAND.—Same treatment. Samples for roads, for glassmaking, concretes, etc. Statistics. Photographs of sandhills near Lake Michigan are of much interest on account of their effects on forests and of forests on them. They are now disappearing.

FOSSILS.—Indiana exhibits in regular order on a line from Richmond to Evansville; the several strata of rocks from the lower Silurian through the Ordovician, Devonian, subcarboniferous and carboniferous to the Permian. Several localities are famous throughout the world as having the richest of beds of fossils. From Richmond to Madison these are Lower Silurian; at Waldron they are Upper Silurian; at Crawfordsville they are subcarboniferous; at Bloomington and many points south from there geodes in great number and variety are to be found. All these should be as thoroughly represented as the space will permit.

MINERALS.—Our species and varieties of minerals should be completely represented; a few of them, as sulfid of iron, are of commercial importance.

GLACIAL PERIOD.—This covers most of the State; nowhere is it susceptible of finer illustration than in Indiana. Its minerals, of course, are of accidental distribution. Our many hundreds of lakes are of glacial origin and constitute a very marked scenic feature; they are in size from twenty miles in circuit to extinct lakes, overgrown, if they had no outlets, by tamarac swamps, if they had, by ordinary deciduous forests; our moraines, lakes, swamps, drift hills, etc., should all be illustrated by photographs; the abundant glacial striae, etc., by specimens.

FOSSIL MAMMALS.—These offer an inviting field. A complete mastodon is in the Earlham museum. Also a Castoroides Ohioensis, the only one in existence.

If loans could be arranged for with all the museums of the State, an exhibit could be made that would educate on these subjects in a manner otherwise impossible.

Stock and Farming Resources

Charles Downing.

A golden opportunity for exploiting Indiana's live stock and farming resources will come in the centennial year of 1916. While the cities of the State abound in manufacturing enterprises, the fact remains that Indiana is first of all in output and wealth immeasurably rich in farming and its allied industries. And the wealth of Indiana along agricultural lines is steadily forging ahead. More ground is

Indiana-Bred Horses. Interior of Coliseum, Indiana State Fair Grounds

being brought under cultivation, more bushels to the acre are coming from better farming methods, more live stock is being produced year by year, and these factors will for generations to come give Indiana farm activities a long lead over any other line of industry within the State.

United States Government census returns for 1912 show that farming is the greatest contributor to the nation's prosperity. In 1912 these returns showed the farms yielded $9,532,000,000 in products. First in the list was animal products, $3,395,000,000; animals sold, $1,930,000,000; then came corn with $1,759,000,000. Indiana has been a heavy contributor to this great volume of the country's wealth.

In 1912 the State had 642,848 horses, against 596,834 in 1900.

In 1911 the State had 964,768 cattle, a steady growth year by year both in number and in higher qualities of blood.

In 1912 Indiana had 73,351 mules, 783,486 sheep and 1,960,700 hogs.

In 1911 Indiana had 16,955,364 fowls in its poultry flocks, which produced 69,446,498 dozen eggs.

The above figures are quoted as evidence that Indiana has immeasurable resources to draw upon for a centennial exposition.

Model Dairy Barn, Acton, Indiana.   Otto R. Lieber

It has been suggested that the Indiana State Board of Agriculture offer the following plan for celebrating the centennial with a great exposition of the State's farming resources along these lines:

That the usual Indiana State Fair in 1916 be abandoned.

That the Indiana State Fair grounds be turned over rent free to a commission to be named by the Legislature, or some other authority, or, if thought desirable, that the exposition of live stock and farm products be placed under the charge of the State Board of Agriculture because of its experience in this direction.

That in general character the centennial exposition of stock and farming resources be a modified form of the Indiana State Fair, spread over a period of weeks, as follows:

First Week—Exposition of Horses and Mules.

Second Week—Exposition of Beef and Dairy Cattle, and Dairy products.

Third Week—Exposition of Sheep and Swine.

Fourth Week—Exposition of Poultry, Fruits, Field and Garden products, Manufactured and Home-made Pure Food products.

Indiana Guernsey Herd. Prize-winning cow. Otto R. Lieber, Acton, Indiana

During the entire period of the exposition that displays of machinery, automobiles, arts and crafts, oils, coal, stone, woods, brick and other Indiana building material be given.

That through the exposition period eminent authorities on farming subjects give educational lectures and addresses; that band concerts and other wholesome entertainment be provided.

The exposition as outlined would be of immense educational value not only to the people of the farms, but to those of the city, who are practically unacquainted with the farming and natural resources of their State, and to visitors who would attend from other States.

The exposition would also be an inspiration to Indiana people to strive for still greater accomplishment in developing the State's resources, in improving the blood of herds and flocks, in obtaining larger and better yields from farm lands.

The Indiana State Fair has ample ground room, transportation facilities and other equipment for such an exposition. But to give these displays on adequate scale two or three additional buildings would be necessary—a cattle barn, a building for manufactured products, a poultry house.

These buildings would have to be provided for out of appropriations by the Legislature, as the State Board of Agriculture does not have sufficient financial resources upon which to draw for the purpose. These additional buildings should be of permanent character so that they could in years to come be utilized for State Fair purposes.

Should this or a similar exposition plan be adopted and the needed buildings erected, the State could reimburse itself for its outlay of money by charging the usual State Fair admission and exhibitors' entry fees, the profits above the exposition's cost and operating expenses to go back into the State treasury.

This plan for a Centennial exposition would accomplish at least four important results: It would exploit the State's resources on a great and comprehensive scale; it would enable the State to commemorate its one hundredth anniversary at moderate, if any, cost; it would give the Indiana State Fair some buildings greatly needed if it is in years to come to measure up to the purposes for which the Legislature created it in 1851; it would set the State before the American people as a commonwealth of culture, progress and wealth.

Manufactures, Commerce and Trade

Edward A. Rumely.

A centennial exposition for the State of Indiana is especially desirable at this time, and if carried through with emphasis sufficient to reach every citizen in the State, it would help us to bind together our State population and strengthen the feeling of unity and common membership in our political organization centralized at Indianapolis.

No group can work effectively together unless its constituent units feel themselves strongly as members of the same body. Indiana lacks a feeling of unity because the settlement of the State did not focus and radiate from a common center.

Our transportation systems run east and west and have divided the State into units that belong to different centers: in the north, Chicago; in the south and west, St. Louis; in the east, Cincinnati. The fact that we have no single newspaper reaching all the parts of the State, able to unify public opinion upon those issues with which our people must deal as a political unit, is a proof of this lack of common center.

A centennial exhibit will bring before our eyes a picture of our development up to the present time and it will help give a feeling of unity; also a retrospect showing the continuity of growth up to the present will lead the thought of the people to the things we are to achieve for ourselves, for our State, and for our Nation. Standards consciously set and recognized are more easily achieved.

An exposition in Indiana ought to be particularly successful, for Indiana is, in a way, a focus point for the entire Nation. Geographically its location is central to the United States. The lines of settlement have gone from the east to the west and practically the entire stream of immigration for the Mississippi Valley and the country beyond has passed through this State. The transportation of goods is still predominatingly east and west, going through Indiana.

The center of population for the whole United States has been within the limits of the State of Indiana since 1890. It is now located at a point within eighty miles of Indianapolis. It will always be easier to bring together all the citizens of the country at the center of population than in any other place.

In point of economic development, Indiana is typical of the Nation. It began in the pioneer days, one hundred years ago, in the

(Loaned by A. E. Leavitt, Harriman, Tennessee

Tunnel Mill, near Vernon, Indiana, erected about 1830. Operated at first by huge overshot wheel, later by turbine. One of the finest of its kind in the early days. Flour was shipped from it by water to Cincinnati and Pittsburg

primitive agricultural condition. Forests alternated with vast areas of virgin prairie, to the mastery and exploitation of which the energies of the first fifty to sixty years were devoted, but as the virgin fertility was depleted, methods of farming had to be changed. From the wheat growing of the frontier State, our farming has been modified and taken in a wide variety of products, representative in the largest way of the mixed agriculture of the present day. Ninety per cent. of the entire population was, in the beginning, supported on the farm. Gradually cities grew and industries arose, that drew a larger and

An Indiana-made Tractor, drawing 14 Indiana-made Plows

larger percentage of the population into industrial pursuits, and today, out of every thousand inhabitants, only three hundred remain on the farm.

The industries of Indiana represent a later phase of manufacture. We have highly manufactured products, such as agricultural implements, vehicles, automobiles, engines, sewing machines, etc., all of which are most characteristic of our whole Nation. Also in the output of primary products, Indiana can well typify American achievement. Steel can be produced in great quantities, and at Gary at a cost unequaled elsewhere in the world. At Whiting petroleum is refined into its thousand products and sent broadcast to the world.

As shown above, Indiana is in a transition stage. Its development from the primitive agricultural State to the modern, complex organization with vast factories and industries and its network of transportation is typical of what has gone on and what is taking place in the United States as a whole.

Our Eastern States have become increasingly manufacturing centers; our Western States are still largely agricultural in their interests. Indiana stands midway. Memories of its earlier conditions still linger in the minds of many of its citizens and help them to under-

The Center of Population in the United States, Bloomington, Indiana

stand the interests and view-points of the West. Indiana has furnished more settlers for the Mississippi Valley and the Western States, than any other one State in the Nation, and also through personal contact with these thousands of people do they get an understanding of the forceful Western spirit, which is asserting itself more and more in American public life.

In their desire for future achievement lies the understanding of the East. The highly organized industrial production with its large wage-earning population has forced before it in cities and in State organizations distinctly modern social problems; the capital, the machinery, the finance, the problems of management of our industries, are similar to those of the East, and through that we can understand and sympathize with the efforts of the older States.

Indiana has opportunity and duty more than any other State of crystallizing the economic, social and political forms through which the Nation shall develop during the next generation.

An exposition well managed and planned can help us to understand one another and act as a whole.

This centennial exhibit should be carried into every public school

Old State Bank Building, Brookville, Indiana. One of the first banks in the State

throughout the State. School children and the youth should be drawn into the work of preparation for the exhibit. Newspapers should coordinate, so that the material would become a vital factor in the thought and feeling of everyone within the borders of our State. The records created should be established in permanent form in photographs and charts and reports so as to be available years after the exhibit itself is over.

If handled in this way our centennial exhibit would be the cause of our becoming conscious in a large way of our duties and work as citizens during the next generation. It would be well worth a million dollars and should have the full coöperation of everyone.

SUGGESTIONS FOR EXHIBITS.

AGRICULTURE.

A log house with the entire equipment of the earliest days, including weapons and other hunting implements of the pioneers. This to be reproduced in exact form.

A complete set of agricultural tools.

Charts showing the date and progress of the State survey, the laying out of the roads and the products in the 40's and 50's. Maps and charts showing the location of earliest settlements, villages and first cities. Interesting manuscript and records of the activity of that period.

TRADES.

The earliest log cabin was the center of industry as well. Industry was domestic, and most trades centered around the home. The exhibit should include tools, products and records of earliest industrial work as carried on in pioneer homes and in the earliest settlements and villages. The log cabin was not only the center of agriculture and industry, but also the home. The exhibit could be arranged to show the changes that have transformed home life to its standard of today. In this connection the exhibits of schools, running from the little country school with its three months a year course, that first took the child from the home, to our modern city school system.

WOMAN.

This line of argument might culminate in an effort to give symbolic expression to the highest conception of what the home should be. At the Conservation Congress, nothing attracted more attention than the model cottage, which was an attempt to typify, in a hasty way, a few of the materials and mechanical appliances of home life. Our exhibit should be broadly an attempt to bring in the higher and more personal relations of the home.

The life and work of woman has undergone, during the last century, what is probably the most profound social change the world has ever known. This drama has taken place in a peculiarly complete way within our own State from the transformation of the mother in the log cabin who wove and spun and made soap, educated her children, practising and preserving the basic arts and trades, to the factory worker, stenographer, the mistress in the home of leisure.

This development, if properly represented in an exhibit, would be of absorbing interest just now when everyone seems to be thinking of the position which woman is occupying in our society. Suggestions for presenting the personal and spiritual changes as well as the material aspects of the development in a symbolic way should be ready for presentation to the chairman of the committee.

MODERN CONDITIONS.

The University of Purdue should be able to project a picture of four or five modern farms to show the present state of our agriculture. The models of the most efficient units to be used for the future. In the neighborhood of our cities truck marketing and fruit gardening must make more and more progress. Dairying to supply milk, meat and butter is essential both to the support of our population and the greater prosperity of our farms.

The modern agricultural implement owes a considerable share of its development to Indiana. Some of the earliest and most successful experiments on reapers, plows, binders, clover hullers and engines have taken place within this State. Exhibits of these tools, with charts and photographs showing their work could be included.

Exhibits showing the work and extent of the other principal industries could be secured so as to present in an interesting way subject-matter that has not been brought together before. Maps and charts of transportation to show the volume and direction of movement.

The two State universities should display their work as carried on at present, including an analysis of the future work and earning power of their students, the bearing of their work upon the industries, and especially the agriculture of the State of Indiana. In working out this exhibit, it is quite probable that a better understanding of their function would gain hold throughout the State, and those in charge would be forced, as well, to realize more fully their relations to the people of this State who support the institutions.

Finally, a complete picture of the relations of our State government and its work, its institutions and its bearing upon the citizens should be made an important part of the exhibit; because more and more, work that exceeds the power of individuals or of corporations is arising. Modern knowledge and modern tools have created demands which can be realized only through the State. And our connection and our dependence upon our State organization must become clearer to us if it is to perform its work sufficiently.

Transportation

Clarence A. Kenyon.

An hundred years ago Indiana was a wilderness. Indians, hunters and trappers were the only inhabitants. A large part of the State was a forest, and wild beasts and game of every description were abundant; the streams were filled with fish. The only means of transportation was the canoe and the pack horse, the only roads were Indian or animal trails. The history of transportation is the history, in a large measure, of civilization. Roads and civilization go hand in hand, each in a way dependent upon the other. As civilization advances roads increase in number and quality, and as the means of easy transportation multiply, civilization increases. This is true of all countries. The transition from the nomadic, semibarbarous, and pastoral manner of life to the commercial, trading, militant, organized civilizations is marked by the means of transportation, which in its broadest sense includes rivers, canoes, railroads, common roads and city streets. The United States has the longest and best roads in the world, and Indiana has its share of such roads, but they are the railroads and they have, in this country been brought to a high degree of perfection, not only in construction, but in methods of upkeep and repair.

As soon as the trappers and hunters began to settle permanently and the pioneers came, land was soon cleared and cultivated. It was absolutely necessary to have some means of transporting their excess products to market. The French came from Canada to the northern part of the State and the Virginians and Kentuckians came in from the south and settled along the streams and rivers. Flatboats made by splitting large trees, tapering them at each end like a sled, were used to float products down the streams; the boat was sold with the produce, as they had no means of getting it back. Next came the keel boat, which was transported by poles. For years communication between Indiana and the older colonies was very precarious. There were no roads into the interior. From Vincennes to the Falls of the Ohio the Indian or buffalo trail was the only semblance to a road. When Indianapolis was laid out there were no roads, and one of the first things the Legislature did was to appropriate money to build roads leading to the capital. One led to Lawrenceburg, another to Madison, another to Jeffersonville, but the appropriation for all of these roads was less than $60,000. So it will be seen that the appropriation was not sufficient to do more than clear the roadway, and do a little grading.

In 1811, Robert Fulton and Robert Livingston put a steamboat on the Ohio River, and in later years a steamboat or two made regular trips to and from Indianapolis. In the early twenties there was great enthusiasm for improved methods of transportation. Over eight millions of dollars were appropriated for the building of canals; and while they carried considerable freight for a time, were abandoned as soon as the railroads came and the money thus appropriated was

The Ox-team was a primitive but sure means of transportation

largely wasted. Our own canal leading to Broad Ripple and beyond, cost the State nearly two millions of dollars and was ultimately sold for about five thousand dollars to private parties. Large sums were appropriated by the Legislature for the purpose of building railroads. The first road which the State attempted to build was to Madison. It would be a long story to tell of the pitiful failure of the State to build and maintain this road and its final passage into the hands of private parties. But the State was growing and needed transportation. The common roads were in very bad condition. When the capital was moved from Corydon to Indianapolis, the State records were hauled by wagons, at the speed of ten or twelve miles a day.

In those days the nearest grist mill to Indianapolis was sixty miles.

Some enterprising citizens established a line of wagons from the Ohio River to the interior. These wagons had a wide bed and were covered with canvas. This was the only way to transport freight. For passengers and mail, stage lines were operated. These stages were great clumsy things, swung on leather springs, hauled by four or six horses. When the weather was bad they frequently stuck in the mud and the passengers would have to help get them out.

Packet Governor Morton, on the first trip up White River in 1860

During the time of Monroe, Clay and Calhoun the problem of internal improvements was one of the burning questions. Agitation was great, not only in Indiana but all over the country. As a result, Congress provided for the construction of the Cumberland or National road, which crossed Indiana from Richmond on the east to Terre Haute on the west. It was never entirely completed and was finally turned over to the States and local authorities. Most of the railroads were built in the forties and fifties, but many of them were projected years before. From 1830 to 1835, there was a great awakening of the public roads spirit in the United States. The people of

Indiana caught the fever and the Legislature of 1835 authorized surveys of six important groups, the first, for railroad or turnpike, from Madison via Indianapolis to Crawfordsville and LaFayette; the second, from Crawfordsville via Greencastle, Bloomington and Salem to New Albany; third, for a railroad from Evansville to Vincennes; fourth, for a railroad from Vincennes to Terre Haute; fifth, macadamized turnpike road from New Albany via Greenville, Paoli and Mt. Pleasant to Vincennes; sixth, to complete the surveys and estimates on the Lawrenceburg and Indianapolis Railway. Many charters

"The Pioneer." First gasoline motor vehicle constructed in the United States. Now in the Smithsonian Institution at Washington. Built by Elwood Haynes, Kokomo, Indiana

were granted, but the money was not forthcoming, and many of the roads were not built. As the railroads began to multiply in the forties and fifties, the necessity for common roads seemed to the people to be less; and it was not for some time after the war that the building of highways was commenced under the assessment and gravel road plans. In all these later plans the State has been left out. No appropriations were granted, no highway engineer or State aid of any kind was provided for, and the era of extreme localization was introduced. Every township has a number of road officers as well as every county,

The Indianapolis Motor Speedway, which holds the World's record for 500 miles, the average rate per hour for that distance being 78.74 miles

mostly without scientific knowledge or experience as road engineers or builders. And yet, with the great abundance of gravel and limestone there is in the State a very considerable mileage of roads has been built, but mostly poorly built and all inadequately maintained.

In 1894, the first interurban was built, and in the last dozen years many lines of interurban roads have been constructed in Indiana. These roads furnished a new convenience to the agricultural communities, and the people again began to feel that it was not necessary to have first-class country highways.

The great advance in highway construction and maintenance that has taken place, and is taking place in other States and nations, has impressed and is every day more and more impressing the people of Indiana with the great necessity for increased economical transportation. The coming of the automobile and the motor truck, and their ever-increasing efficiency, is making it evident that our highways must be of better construction, and more perfectly maintained, or our State will fall behind in the race for supremacy. Few factories nowadays can endure unless a railroad switch runs to the factory, because the manufacturer cannot afford to pay the cost of wagon transportation from the factory to the railroad. If this be true, how can the products of the farm stand the present great cost of twenty cents per ton per mile from the farm to the railroad, and from market centers back to the farm, when with hard roads the same products can be hauled for ten cents per ton per mile, or one-half the cost? The railroads now haul the products of the farm for three-fourths of one cent per ton per mile, or one-twenty-fifth of hauling to the railroad.

One of the greatest problems of life today is conservation and economy; and so in any plan for the advancement of a State or its people, this great problem of transportation must be met and answered. The State must help. Agricultural schools and increased soil fertility will increase the amount of produce raised to feed the rapidly increasing millions, but of what avail is it unless we find an easier and cheaper way to transport these products from where they are plenty to where they are scarce; in other words, from the country to the towns and cities. The problem is so great that it almost staggers the imagination.

What greater thing could the State do at its centennial exposition than present this problem and its remedy to the people of the State. It is easily within the power of the proposed exposition, not only to show to the people, by means of pictures, maps, materials and models, the method and growth of transportation from the earliest times,

"The Hoosier Limited." Showing Up-to-Date Railway Transportation

down through the ages, from the earth road and the pack horse, to the famous Appian Way that still exists after more than two thousand years of use, to the "flat" and "keel" and canal boats, the stage coach, the prairie schooner, the locomotive, the interurban, the automobile, and in addition to all this, a vision of the wonders that are almost within our grasp. We must in a way anticipate the future; we need the very great improvements that are now almost within our grasp. The Japanese have a proverb, "One look is better than a thousand words;" and this great exposition, if properly presented in "looks" will teach our people that which will be worth more to the State than the entire cost of the exposition. Let us do it.

OLD CONSTITUTIONAL ELM.
Corydon, Indiana

(Loaned by H. J. Friedly

Under this tree the first constitution of Indiana was adopted. Its spreading branches covered an area 120 feet in diameter. Still alive, but showing evidence of decay

How to Awaken General Interest and Participation

Lew M. O'Bannon.

In proportion to the number interested and made active participants in any plan devised, will the celebration become a success and of largest benefit to all the people. To attain these ends it is suggested that there should be:

I. A Campaign of Educational Agitation.

1. A systematic method of advertising the celebration should be inaugurated through the newspapers of the State, setting forth the scope and purposes of the proposed celebration. To this end appropriate copy should be prepared by a competent person or committee selected for this purpose.

2. An effort might properly be made to get various organizations of men and women, both State and local, to place the stamp of approval upon such plans for the celebration as may be worked out by the Centennial Celebration Committee.

3. If it would not involve too much labor and too heavy cost it would certainly be a great help if a booklet could be prepared containing in brief what we might properly call an "Inventory" of Indiana's achievements in a hundred years, to be used in all the schools of the State, using, in a limited way, pictures of such historic scenes and of public and private property covering the entire century, as would illustrate the tremendous progress made in all lines of business in that time. Such a compilation might be made sufficiently valuable and attractive that it could be sold in large numbers over the State, thus serving the double purpose of creating widespread interest in the proposed celebration and creating a fund to help pay necessary expenses, at least in a small measure.

In this little volume could be used some of the choicest things that have been said in eulogy of our State, both in prose and verse, by Indiana writers, thus sharpening the appetites of the people for what is in prospect. Arouse the pride of Hoosiers in the splendid achievements of themselves and their ancestors during the century and the work of making the celebration a success is made easier.

4. There might be some system of prizes, or premiums, offered at the celebration upon exhibits with a plan, in some line or lines, which would admit articles of production by townships and counties. Especially might this be used to advantage in agricultural counties.

II. Local Celebrations.

1. A date should be fixed for appropriate exercises in all parts of the State—if deemed practical, in all the townships—literary and musical, and possibly an exhibit of articles of superior quality in

A Primitive Habitation. Let the children in the schools be told again and again the stories of early Hoosier life--its dangers and privations calling for the sturdiest heroism

certain lines of production peculiar to such localities, according to a program as nearly uniform as practical for the entire State. By this means the largest number of the people of the State could be brought in touch with the nutritive influences that have been potent factors in the development of the industrial, educational, literary and religious interests of the commonwealth during the first hundred years of its existence.

2. Every locality in the State could be amply prepared for these local celebrations by means of instruction through the schools during the three years intervening between now and 1916. This plan could

be enlarged upon and extended according to the degree of interest developed and the facilities available in various places.

3. It might also be well to hold similar exhibitions and celebrations at all the county seats of the nintey-two counties of the State, especially at such places as Corydon, Vincennes, Lafayette, Battleground, etc., where historical events of State importance have occurred.

History occupies a high place in our best plans for successful education, and by giving Hoosiers a somewhat clear, though brief,

A Beautiful Road through the Canadian Rocky Mountains

Another Beautiful Road over Bear Wallow Hill in Brown County, Indiana

look into the past history of Indiana, I doubt not their sympathies can be warmed for the celebration proposition.

Emerson spoke an important truth when he said: "There is a relation between the hours of our life and the centuries of time." The past is ours as well as the present, and upon the proper and wise use of both depends our success in the future.

These are only suggestions, and they are modestly submitted in the hope that they may at least lead to something helpful in the efforts being made to lay the plans for a successful centennial celebration in Indiana in 1916.

Convention Hall, Indianapolis

Henry R. Danner and L. H. Lewis.

After months of careful study and investigation, a committee representing the several commercial organizations of Indianapolis has decided to inaugurate a campagn to raise funds with which to erect a large coliseum or convention hall. This campaign will be started as soon as arrangements can be made. The committee has sent out a call for "volunteers" and the rosponses indicate that the movement has struck a very hearty chord and will be consummated with celerity.

No movement ever started in Indianapolis with a better setting. The conditions are ripe. Every citizen realizes that a coliseum is a prime necessity. Thousands of visitors could be attracted here annually and scores of meritorious propositions could be staged if Indianapolis possessed such a building. The investigation in other cities conducted by the committee pointed out conclusively that one of the things necessary for the success and welfare of any city today is a convention hall large enough to accommodate any gathering. It is a potent factor in community growth and development.

Indianapolis is ideally located as a convention center. Its hotel accommodations are ample, its transportation facilities cannot be excelled anywhere, while it is within forty miles of the center of population of the United States. Statistics show that conventions held here attract more members of the organizations than in other cities because of the first class accommodations in every respect. That is what has made Indianapolis known the world over as the "Premier Convention City."

Without a coliseum Indianapolis is not in a position to entertain large conventions, and especially those that hold exhibits in connection with their convention. This class of conventions is the best from the "mercenary dollar and cent standpoint." Indianapolis could easily obtain one of the big national political conventions if it had a building where the gathering could be held.

All of these conditions have served to awaken Indianapolis to this great need until there is absolutely no question but that the campaign for funds could be carried to completion speedily and with ease. Every person realizes that a coliseum is a business necessity. It is more than that. A coliseum in Indianapolis would do more to advance the interests of the entire city than any other single enterprise.

Present indications are that the campaign for funds will not be of lengthy duration. The public pulse has been felt and the diagnosis given indicates a quick consummation of the project. From every part of the city has come "I will help you. Let us start now." The

An adequate Convention Hall in Indianapolis is a pressing need both for the city and State, which must and will be met by the public-spirited citizenship of Indianapolis in ample time for the Centennial Celebration

spirit manifest in every section is indicative that "all is well" and that the enterprise will not fall by the wayside.

The coliseum will be built and ready for occupancy when the time arrives for the celebration of Indiana's one-hundredth birthday in 1916. "Home pride" makes every Indianapolitan feel that he must do his share to make the celebration a tremendous success and to make it so the city must have a coliseum to house at least a part of the exhibits that will be made in connection with the celebration, and as a meeting place for the big gatherings that will be held.

The coliseum will be built with a view of serving all of the purposes of such a building. It will be large and roomy and a model of architecture. It will be centrally located and easily accessible from every direction.

Indianapolis realizes that "it must" and when it believes that "it must" the expression is quickly supplemented by "it will." The committee in charge of the movement has received hearty encouragement all down the line and it feels that now is the accepted time to stage the movement to obtain the funds. This will be a "citizens movement" participated in by the entire city, and one that will be crowned with success.

Going Back Home

Wilbur D. Nesbit.

Indiana is a State where Destiny sits on the doorstep, and Opportunity yanks the bellpull off the door jamb and then tells the man to come along; where Fame goes through the streets with an armful of laurel chaplets; where Ambition is pushed to one side by men who tell it to go overleap itself, according to Shakespeare, but that for themselves they have some duties to perform.

The Call of Duty is heard there with the naked ear; Duty never has to yell through a megaphone, talk on its fingers or write follow-up letters.

The Nation began drafting Indiana's population as soon as the State was settled, and Hoosierdom has made history so fast that the historians have never caught up with events.

It isn't any wonder that all over this and several other countries Hoosiers are marking in red ink the dates covering Home Coming Week.

We're all going back home.

And there's this blessed thing about Indiana—the people who who greet us will be just as glad to see us home again as we will be to get there.

It is a wonderful thing for us, this Home Coming Week.

It broadens us and betters us; it sets our feet in the old paths: we breathe the old air; we see the old flowers, and the old hills, and the old people—God bless them!

Whether we drop off the train at the little way station and find our way up the street on each side of which roses peep through the broken palings of sleepy fences, whether we climb into a shiny trap and speed along the boulevard, whether we pile into a touring car and roll out along a pike between fields from which drift heavy odors of clover and hay, over the bridge beneath which grows mint that spices the twilight, through the woods where shadow fairies dance among the trees, to bring us up at the old gate opening on the old walk between the beds of marigold and phlox and sweet william and four-o'clock—it's home.

And home is where the heart is, and the heart is where home is, now and forevermore, amen!

Welcome Home! in 1916

And if it be daylight, the front door will be open, and the old walls and floors and pictures will be giving us welcome; and if it be dark the front door will be open and the mellow lamplight will fling a pathway of its own out into the shadows for us.

And next day there'll be the old boys—and the girls who are ever young—and the old times will be lived over again, and Home Coming

Return again to the Hoosier haunts of childhood. Lingering in your memory may be the picture of a "homey" old place like this. Perhaps it may all be changed now, but you can at least tread again the sacred ground

Week shall be as Fourth of July and Christmas and New Years and Thanksgiving and all other good days rolled into one.

And the memories we have cherished shall live for us in reality once more, the old songs shall have a newer sweetness—even the old stories shall have a newer and fresher tang to them.

The haunts of boyhood, that call to us ever out of the silences, and in the clamor of alien streets, shall be ours once more.

"The Big Woods." Does your memory hark back to the day when every Hoosier community had its "Big Woods" of beech, hickory, giant oak and poplar? What a charm of mystery there was in following the meandering path, amongst towering trees and tangled thickets, alive with the songs and chatter of wild creatures

A Little Hoosier Church on the Hillside. In your travels abroad to see picturesque and secluded shrines, did you see anything more charmingly artistic than this?

When the Hoosiers go home there'll be shaking of hands
And the eloquent hush that the heart understands,
And the smile that's a sigh, and the sigh that's a smile
When they stand and think back every wonderful while,
And repeople the town, and undo every change
Till in fancy, at least, it no longer is strange.

When the Hoosiers go home there'll be welcoming cheers
And they'll laugh in reply till they laugh out their tears,
For, you know, though forgetfulness comes when we roam
There's a surge of old memories when we go home,
When we wonder where are all the friends we knew there—
But we know, and our lips will not frame the word "Where?"

When the Hoosiers go home—why, the roads and the trees
And the outspreading fields, and the hum of the bees
Will be welcoming them! And the blue of the sky
Will be bluer than ever in days long gone by!
And the sunshine and shade will be flecking the grass
Like a mirroring gladness that laughs as they pass.

When the Hoosiers go home—O it's splendid to know
That you never lose touch with the long, long ago;
That the old gate still swings, and the door is flung wide,
And that folks are your friends and your fellows beside!
There'll be songs that are sweet as the blossomy foam
Of the orchards abloom, when the Hoosiers go home.

SUPPLEMENT

Quotations from a Few Letters Relating to the Proposed Centennial Celebration in 1916

DAVID STARR JORDAN, President Leland Stanford Junior University.

"Permit me to acknowledge your kind letter of November 26th. I am very greatly interested in your proposed Centennial Celebration, and I shall do whatever I can at this long range, toward helping in the matter."

JOSEPH SWAIN, President Swarthmore College.

"I have your letter of November 26th enclosing resolutions concerning the contemplated Indiana Centennial Celebration. I am always interested in everything that takes place in my native State, and I thank you for giving me information concerning this movement. You have a good and representative committee and I think the plans are safe in their hands."

LIEUTENANT-GOVERNOR GORDON, Cincinnati, Ohio.

"As one of the ex-Hoosiers who has always kept in touch with Indiana and her people, and has a great affection for both, I desire to express the hope that you will have a Home-Coming feature in connection with the Centennial, in order that we ex-Hoosiers may feel on visiting the Centennial that we have a part in it. I am sure that such a feature if carried out, will be a great success."

CAPTAIN JAMES B. CURTIS, New York City.

"It affords me pleasure to endorse the plan of a Centennial Celebration in 1916 by the State of Indiana. When a resident there it was always a privilege for me to do everything possible for the good name of Indianapolis and Indiana. In leading the old Indianapolis Light Artillery to victory for fifteen years in succession, much was accomplished along this line. Since leaving you it has been a delight to me to organize the Indiana Society in New York and give dinners which always attracted much attention. I sincerely hope that you will push this scheme to a successful conclusion."

ROBERT JUDSON ALEY, President of the University of Maine.

"I am greatly interested in the Indiana Centennial. As a loyal ex-Hoosier I desire to contribute all that I can for the success of the celebration.

"Indiana in her first hundred years of Statehood, has made for herself a very honorable place. Her public institutions, her laws, her judiciary, her public men, her schools, her colleges, and her literature have taken high rank. It is very important that she should pause for a moment and celebrate in a fitting manner her achievements. Such a celebration would not only be a fitting end to a great century, but also a proper introduction to the still greater century which is to follow. The many Hoosiers who are living and working in other States would hail with joy the opportunity to come home. They would rejoice to see a celebration worthy of the great State they love so well. Each of us loves his adopted State as he loves his wife, but he loves Indiana as he loves his mother."

THE INDIANAPOLIS CHAMBER OF COMMERCE.

"The Indianapolis Chamber of Commerce commends the highly patriotic and unselfish motives of your committee and assures you that it has the heartiest and best wishes of this organization in your endeavor to promulgate successfully the movement looking toward a proper observance of Indiana's one hundreth birthday in 1916.

"Indiana is a wonderful State. Her growth and development during the last century have been marvelous. How fitting it would be to have a joint exhibit and celebration in 1916 showing the progress made along all lines of community life.

"The movement under your auspices is truly meritorious. It deserves to succeed. The celebration as proposed and tentatively outlined by your committee would unquestionably be a revelation to many and act as an incentive to raise the standard of ideals, and foster that spirit of good fellowship that is always manifest in the citizenship of Indiana.

"Staged on a high plane with the educational feature predominating throughout, we believe such an exhibit and celebration would attract thousands of strangers and serve as a means of bringing back home those citizens who have drifted to other shores.

"We appreciate your display of fealty and loyalty to old Indiana, and hope that the success, your efforts so richly deserve, will be yours."

Illustrations Showing Progress of the State in Educational, Industrial and Other Fields

Newer Buildings of Colleges in Indiana

Notre Dame University

Franklin College

Library Building, Indiana University

Hendricks Memorial Library, Hanover College

Butler College

Meharry Hall, DePauw University

Pictures Illustrative of Progress and Development of the State in Various Fields

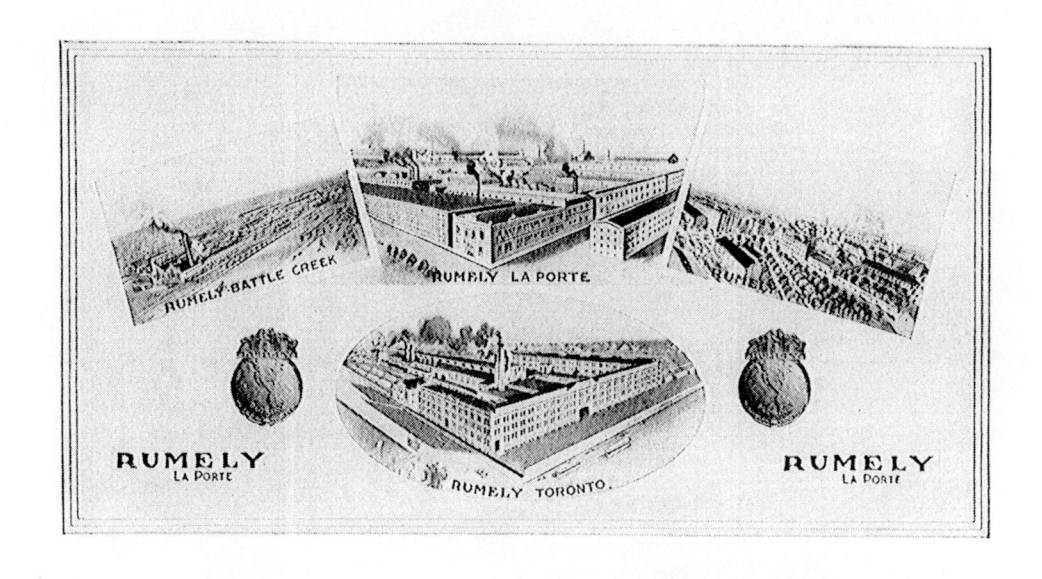

The Beginning

The Present Studebaker Plant

1876

Laboratory first established on Pearl Street. The site is now occupied by the rear of the
Indianapolis Chamber of Commerce Building

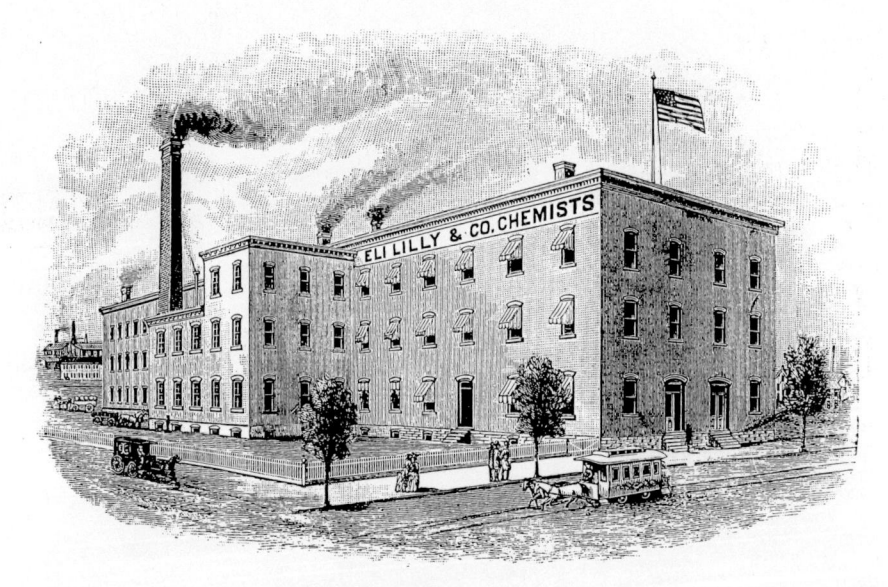

1881

ELI LILLY & COMPANY
Pharmaceutical Chemists

Home Office and Laboratories, Indianapolis, Ind.

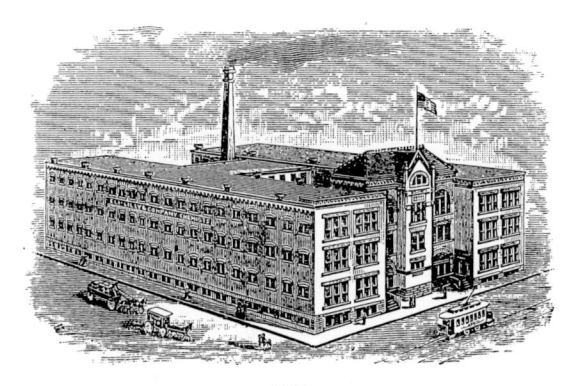

1890

Biological Laboratories, near Greenfield, Ind.
Under Construction, 1913]

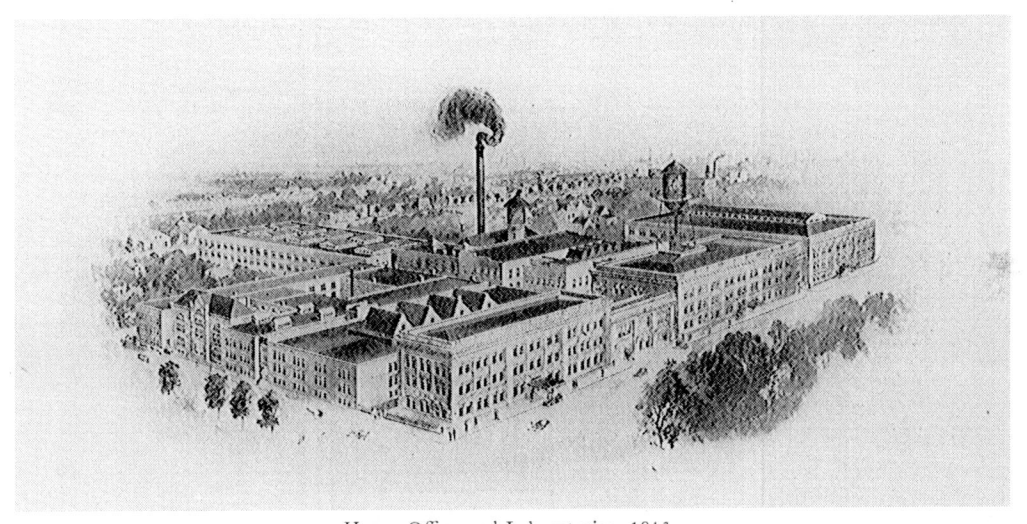

Home Office and Laboratories, 1913

ELI LILLY & COMPANY
Pharmaceutical Chemists

Home Office and Laboratories, Indianapolis Ind.

Branches:
NEW YORK, CHICAGO, ST. LOUIS, KANSAS CITY, NEW ORLEANS

Gary, Indiana.

1. Y. M. C. A. Building   2. New Theater   3. Steel Mills

IN NORTH PENNSYLVANIA ST. 1875

PRESENT SITE 1880–1903.

THE INDIANAPOLIS NEWS

THE INDIANAPOLIS NEWS 1913.

The Indianapolis Star Building

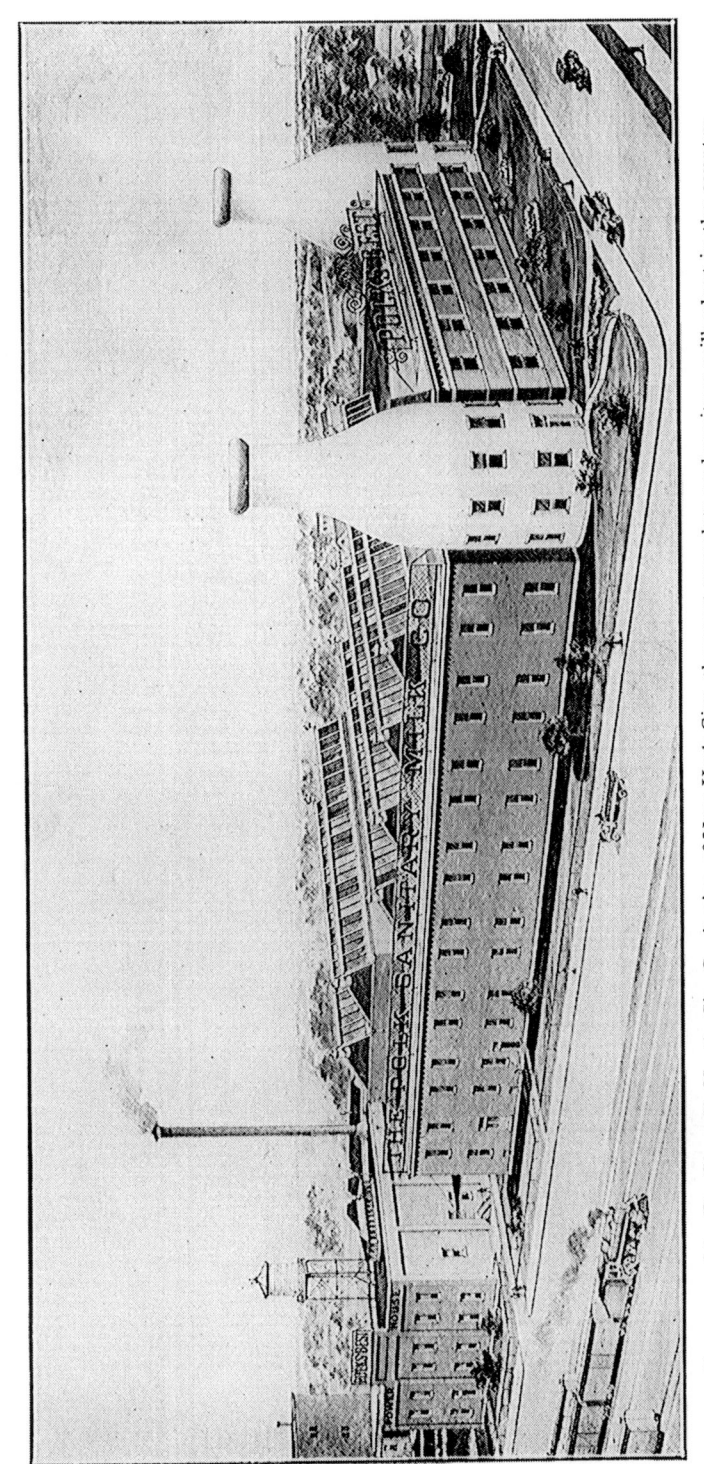

Pronounced by Dr. Chas. E. North, City Sanitarian of New York City, the most complete and sanitary milk plant in the country

NORDYKE & MARMON COMPANY

TODAY

1851

ONE of the oldest and greatest industries of Indiana is Nordyke & Marmon Company of Indianapolis. Founded in 1851, this concern has built up a world-wide business in the manufacture of flour milling machinery, and today the concern is recognized as leading manufacturers in the cereal milling field.

In addition, new laurels have come to the Company in the manufacture of the Marmon Car, which is designed and constructed completely in this factory. As winner of records and trophies in many of the world's greatest contests on track and road as well as in its records in the hands of owners, the Marmon occupies an enviable position among the best cars of Europe and America.

ONE OF THE WORLD-FAMED GROUP OF MARMON TROPHIES

Making History in Indiana

"National" Car Establishing World's Record for 500 Miles

A National built in Indianapolis by the National Motor Vehicle Company, defeated all comers from the entire world in history's hardest race, May 30, 1912, on the famous Indianapolis Motor Speedway—500 miles in 381 minutes and 6 seconds. Never before had a man or machine traveled so fast for that distance. You will agree that although you may not be a devotee of the motor car racing sport you are well enough informed on motor cars to know that when a car withstands this terrific speed for 500 miles, straining every ounce of power and ever fiber of strength, it is unimpeachable proof of the car's quality and stamina. If there is a flaw or weakness in a car it will come out in such a white heat analytical test. This triumph on the Indianapolis Speedway in 1912, of an Indiana made car, is not only a splendid testimonial to the maker of the car, but an achievement in which all Hoosiers take pride.

National Motor Vehicle Co.
INDIANAPOLIS
Sales Branch, 426 North Capitol Avenue

Traction Terminal Building and Station of Indianapolis. Largest of its kind in the country. Six hundred trains arrive and depart from this station daily

Claypool Hotel, Indianapolis

Washington Hotel, Indianapolis

Two Indiana Health Resorts of National Reputation

French Lick Hotel

West Baden Hotel